COURAGE FOR LIFE

STUDY GUIDE

DISCOVER A LIFE FULL OF CONFIDENCE, HOPE, AND OPPORTUNITY!

ANN WHITE

Courage For Life Study Guide
© 2018 by Ann White

Ann White
Courage For Life
1000 Whitlock Avenue
Suite 320-134
Marietta, GA 30064
CourageForLife.org

Published by Insight International, Inc.
contact@freshword.com
www.freshword.com
918-493-1718

Unless otherwise noted, Scripture quotations are taken from the NEW AMERICAN STANDARD BIBLE®, © The Lockman Foundation 1960, 1962, 1963, 1968, 1971, 1972, 1973,
1975, 1977, 1995. Used by permission.

Scripture quotations marked ESV are from the THE ENGLISH STANDARD VERSION. © 2001 by Crossway Bibles, a division of Good News Publishers.

Scripture quotation marked KJV is taken from the King James Version of the Bible.

ISBN: 978-1-943361-40-3

Printed in the United States of America.

DEDICATION

To those brave souls who faced their fears and encouraged me to provide this study guide resource to be used in tandem with the book *Courage For Life,* you inspire me to stay strong.

CONTENTS

INTRODUCTION

Courage begins with one fearless choice. You can make that choice today and allow God to change your life.

Courage is something we all want and need. However, many of us struggle to muster it up. Courage is the ability to take on new challenges and persevere in difficult times. And for those who desire to walk in unwavering faith, courage is the ability to make fearless, wise, and biblical choices—all while trusting God with our circumstances and outcomes.

From the moment we're saved, we embark on the life-changing journey of becoming more like Christ. For many of us, fear hinders the process. I know this was true for me. In fact, I spent years denying my problems and fears even existed, living in a world of dysfunction and isolation. For a very long time, I was afraid to let anyone see the real me. Fear fueled much of my life. Can you relate?

When I found myself in a hotel room in Israel at the end of my rope and headed for divorce, I had no idea I was about to test-drive the courage steps that would lead me to write a book. As I consistently followed these seven steps, day after day, they changed my life. No matter what fearful situation you may be experiencing, these same steps can change your life as well.

When I wrote *Courage For Life (CFL)*, I outlined a process readers could follow to gain needed courage for everyday life. Shortly after the book released, it was an unexpected blessing to discover that readers here and abroad were coming together to challenge and support one another in making fearless choices and walking in unwavering faith.

Since writing *CFL,* I've been overwhelmed by enthusiastic responses from readers who share how God has used the book to challenge them to open up, share their struggles, and implement courageous choices—and changes. These fearless actions have ultimately allowed many sisters and brothers in Christ to become the courageous children God designed us to be.

Reader Responses:

Courage For Life is a wonderful book! If I had this book in my late twenties to forties, I might have been spared some of the most frightening and hurtful years of my life—despite knowing Jesus personally.

–Sue B.

When I received my book, I felt as though the words on the pages were written just for me. *Courage For Life* resonated with me at a time when I needed it the most!

–Elaine H.

I am emotionally and spiritually moved with each page!

–Julie M.

I wish *Courage For Life* had been on the market ten years ago! Having courage to put up healthy boundaries in relationships and having realistic expectations are areas where I need to take courage to the max! I especially love having the Scripture verses listed with the "Top Twenty Truths That Replace Worldly Lies"!

–Jennifer H.

I firmly believe each Scripture we understand and apply becomes a building block in our personal relationship with God. And, I firmly believe our relationship with God is the ultimate source of courage for our everyday life. Therefore, in studying God's Word, we build the foundation and set the stage for unleashing our God-given courage.

Armed with the knowledge that my friends, loved ones, and readers wanted more, I began teaching *CFL* in my local church and wrote lessons for each week's class. It didn't take long to see God's hand in the process; it became evident that I must turn those weekly lessons into a *Study Guide,* a resource that could take readers on a rich, structured, and practical journey through *CFL* and God's Word. This is the resource you now hold in your hands. Together, we will journey through seven COURAGE steps that can transform your life:

The Seven Steps to COURAGE:

C = **Commit** to Change

O = **Overcome** Obstacles

U = **Uncover** Your True Self

R = **Replace** Worldly Lies with Scriptural Truth

A = **Accept** the Things You Cannot Change

G = **Grasp** God's Love for You

E = **Embrace** a Life of Grace

Over the next twelve weeks, we're going to unpack these seven steps in a way that will challenge you and ultimately change your life. We're going to take practical steps to break down the obstacles currently hindering you from living courageously and pursuing your God-given dreams.

At the start of every lesson, I give you a Courage Quote to ponder. I'm also going to challenge you to memorize a new verse of Scripture every week, verses I fondly call our Courage Verses. This practice will strengthen your ability to face each day with courage and confidence. At the end of each lesson, I review the week's Courage Quote and Courage Verse and provide a place for you to write the Timeless Life Lessons you learned throughout the week.

During this study, some weeks will be more emotionally challenging than others. From time to time, I will ask you to answer sensitive questions; these intense questions are extremely important to your courage journey. If you're like me, you may struggle with answering these. When I was strengthening my courage muscles, I, too, had reservations about penning answers to very delicate questions. Nonetheless, these questions are extremely important to the process, and it's imperative you do your best to answer them.

Therefore, if you come across a sensitive question, one you hesitate to answer on paper, consider journaling your answer in a computer program that can be password protected. If you don't have access to a secure place to journal your answers, share them with God in prayer and ask Him to heal your fears as you move forward in your journey to courage.

Along with this *Study Guide,* you will need a few more things:

1. Your own copy of *Courage For Life (CFL)* (please, no photocopies)

2. Your preferred Bible translation (I primarily use New American Standard Bible [NASB] or English Standard Version [ESV] for Bible study.)

3. Your favorite pen and highlighter

4. Note cards to use for Scripture memorization

5. Your favorite study space for quiet, contemplative reading, writing, studying, and prayer

6. Your preferred Bible commentary for more extensive study (optional)

This *Study Guide* has been developed for both individual and group study. I've also included a Group Study Leader Guide at the back of this study guide, in case you feel called to lead a small group in your home, church, or maybe even your business. And I want to thank you in advance for your desire to lead your group toward courage.

Okay, dear reader, are you ready for a heavy dose of Christ-like courage? There's no better time than now to overcome your fears and strengthen your spiritual growth. I'm so excited you've set aside time to become more courageous in your daily walk with the Lord. It's your turn to see what God has in store for you!

I thank God for you and your courageous heart.

Be strong and courageous! Do not tremble or be dismayed,
for the Lord your God is with you wherever you go.
Joshua 1:9b

HIDING GOD'S WORD IN OUR HEART

God's Word transforms, but only to the depth we engage it and the pace at which we apply it.

If you continue in My word, then you are truly disciples of Mine; and you will know the truth, and the truth will make you free.

–John 8:31b-32

When starting any new venture, we first prepare our mind for the task at hand. When going on a trip, we first grab a map (or, these days, GPS). When setting out on a journey toward courage, the Bible helps with both these fundamental tasks: it prepares our mind for action and serves as our GPS.

Eight years before I began my personal journey through the seven COURAGE steps, I began learning Bible study techniques that enabled me to approach the Bible with boldness and confidence. As a result, I built a firm foundation based on biblical truth, which strengthened my personal relationship with God and prepared me to embrace my God-given courage. That's why I decided to make Bible study basics the first step in our journey to courage.

In John 14:6, Christ reveals He is "the way, and the truth, and the life." In John 17:17, in Christ's final prayer, He asks God to sanctify His followers "in truth" and affirms God's Word "is truth." Therefore, the focus of this first lesson will be studying, interpreting, and applying the truth of God's Word to our life; His Word is the foundation for courage and change.

Day ONE: A Change in Perspective

When we hide God's Word in our hearts and rely on the voice of truth (the Holy Spirit) to guide us, we significantly increase our ability to discern truth, strengthening our courage muscles in the process. That's why, at the start of every lesson, I'm going to challenge you to memorize a new verse of Scripture.

Write this week's Courage Verse, John 8:31b-32, on a note card. Place it where you will see it often and practice memorizing it throughout the week.

Throughout life, we will encounter misunderstandings and misinterpretations of God's Word. While it's impossible to ensure we interpret Scripture with 100 percent accuracy, we can more reliably understand God's truth by approaching the Bible from the proper perspective and consistently implementing the important Bible study steps I teach you in this lesson. You will practice these steps over and over during our twelve weeks together—until you are equipped with a proven method for studying the Word and applying it to your life.

To understand our Bible study steps more fully, let's begin by considering the two primary ways we can approach Scripture: deductively and inductively.

Deductive Bible Study

When we approach God's Word deductively, we begin with a belief we accept as truth and then search Scripture for verses and passages to support our predetermined opinion. For example, growing up, Dad would say, "God helps those who help themselves," and Mom would assure me, "This too shall pass." I heard phrases like these repeated throughout my childhood. Mom read the Bible, and we occasionally went to church, so I assumed these common clichés were biblical truths. Looking for verses to prove these truths would be deductive study. (However, when I learned to study the Bible inductively, I saw these expressions in a different light.)

Take, for example, Jeremiah 29:11: "'For I know the plans that I have for you,' declares the LORD, 'plans for welfare and not for calamity to give you a future and a hope.'" Approaching the Bible deductively, we might locate and recite this passage as reason to believe God wants to make our lives comfortable, easy, and full of happiness. However, that isn't entirely true. In fact, once we learn to read this verse inductively in its proper context, we discover it has little to do with God's desire to make our lives comfortable.

Inductive Bible Study

When we approach God's Word inductively, we begin by applying established Bible study steps, which lead us to discover what we'll call Timeless Life Lessons, truths that can substantiate or transform our beliefs. In other words, we begin with Scripture and learn the truth of God's Word as it applies to what we are experiencing—not the other way around. It's all about asking the right questions.

We must learn to ask questions of each verse of Scripture, such as the following: Who was the message for? When was the message first given? What did the message mean to its original audience? By employing this approach, we put the verse in its proper context and prepare ourselves to discover a more accurate (inductive) interpretation.

Let's study Jeremiah 29:1-10 with an inductive approach. In this verse, we discover the prophet Jeremiah was speaking to Jewish priests, prophets, and people living in Babylon a few short years after they were taken from their homeland into captivity.[1] As we dig further into the meaning of Jeremiah's message, we realize God was telling the Jews to get comfortable in captivity because they were going to be there for approximately sixty more years.

Yes, Jeremiah 29:11 was a message of hope for the Israelites, but not in the way they might have expected. God was ensuring them He had a plan for their future, one that would ultimately bring welfare and hope—but they would have to wait and endure hardship for the time being.

Now that we know the original meaning of this passage for its intended audience, we are able to better understand its meaning for us today. A Timeless Life Lesson for this verse is that God does have plans for us, plans for welfare, not calamity, to give us a future and a hope. But we will still experience hardship and suffering throughout our lives. We must simply be willing to accept God's plans over our plans and trust Him with our future—in spite of our current circumstances, in spite of the not-so-happy aspects of life, and in spite of the fact our future may look very different than we might expect.

Discovering a New Perspective

To accurately learn God's Word of Truth, we must approach the Bible less deductively and more inductively and allow Scripture to reveal truth, which we then accept, treasure, and apply to our lives.

This may sound a bit confusing at first—particularly for those of us who have been deductively reading the Bible for years. If that's you, have no fear; the fact is, most of us start out reading the Bible from that perspective. To break this habit, we must simply implement Four Basic Bible Study Steps and practice, practice, practice—which is exactly what we will be doing together. Now, grab that favorite pen of yours and let's get started.

1. Describe your understanding of the difference between deductive Bible study and inductive Bible study.

   Deductive:

   _____

   _____

   _____

   Inductive:

   _____

   _____

   _____

2. Read the following passages and describe your initial observations:

   Philippians 4:13

   _____

   _____

   _____

---

[1] Frank E. Gaebelein, Geoffrey W. Grogan, Charles L. Feinberg, H.L. Ellison, and Ralph H. Alexander, *The Expositor's Bible Commentary: Isaiah, Jeremiah, Lamentations, Ezekiel.* Vol. 6. (Grand Rapids, MI: Zondervan Publishing House, 1986).

James 2:14, 17

_____

_____

_____

Acts 5:29

_____

_____

_____

3. Journal additional thoughts God has placed on your heart regarding today's topic.

_____

_____

_____

_____

_____

_____

_____

_____

_____

4. Write a prayer to God based on the truth you discovered in these verses.

_____

_____

_____

_____

_____

_____

_____

_____

Day TWO: Pray, Observe, Interpret, and Apply

Begin today's study by practicing this week's Courage Verse, John 8:31b-32.

As we discussed on day 1, we will learn to employ Four Basic Bible Study Steps. This inductive approach will lead you to a more accurate interpretation of God's Word. In time, these steps will become as natural to you as breathing. Just remember to P–O–I–A:

1. **PRAY** as you approach God's Word. Ask the Holy Spirit to guide you into all truth.

2. **OBSERVE** God's Word. Ask questions to discover the meaning: what does the text say?

3. **INTERPRET** God's Word. Ask the question, what does the text mean?

4. **APPLY** God's Word. Ask the question, what do I need to do?

I discuss these Four Basic Bible Study Steps in chapter 14 of *CFL*: "Grasp God's Love for You." We will now expand on these steps, which will prepare you to complete future assignments in this study guide.

Turn to page 164 in *CFL* and read pages 164-165 (beginning at the header "Getting to Know God's Word," on page 164 and ending at the header "God's Love Revealed," on page 165).

1. Describe the role the Bible currently plays in your life.

_____

_____

_____

_____

Now, let's take time to discover what the Bible has to say about the role God intended it to play in our lives.

2. Read the following verses and describe what you learn about God's Word.

2 Timothy 3:16

_____

_____

_____

_____

Hebrews 4:12

_____

_____

_____

_____

Matthew 24:35

_____

_____

_____

_____

Proverbs 4:20-22

_____

_____

_____

_____

Psalm 119:105

_____

_____

_____

_____

3. Journal additional thoughts God has placed on your heart regarding today's topic.

_____

_____

_____

_____

_____

_____

_____

4. Write a prayer to God.

_____

_____

_____

_____

_____

_____

_____

Day THREE: Unpacking the Four Basic Bible Study Steps

Practice this week's Courage Verse, John 8:31b-32. Are you able to recite any of it without looking at your card? Try it and see.

As I mentioned on day 1 of this week's lesson, the best way to establish a pattern of approaching God's Word inductively is to practice, practice, practice. So let's get started by reviewing the Four Basic Bible Study Steps, the P-O-I-A.

Step 1: PRAY AS YOU APPROACH GOD'S WORD

Before we begin, ask the Holy Spirit to guide you into all truth. Preparing our hearts and minds to receive truth from the Bible is the first step we must take each and every time we approach God's Word.

1. Take a few minutes to write a prayer, thanking God for His Word. Ask Him to give you wisdom and discernment as you seek comfort and guidance through the study of Scripture.

_____

_____

_____

_____

Step 2: OBSERVE GOD'S WORD

What does this text say? This question guides the important second step of discovery. The observation step requires we set aside ample time to closely consider the details within and around each passage of Scripture—a critical step that helps us understand what the passage is saying. This will be the most time-consuming step in our Four Basic Bible Study Steps. But, this step is critical to placing each passage in its proper context, which is imperative to proper interpretation. Let's put it this way: the more time you spend on this particular step, the more accurate an interpretation you will get.

Let's take a closer look at Philippians 4:13. On day 1, I asked you to write down your initial observations of this verse. Today, we will approach this verse inductively and work to discover its true meaning. We will search surrounding verses as we answer our observation questions, and this will place Philippians 4:13 in its proper context.

When observing any verse or passage, we must answer six important observation questions: *Who, What, When, Where, Why,* and *How*. These questions prepare us to view God's Word in its proper context, allowing us to more accurately identify a Timeless Life Lesson, which can then be applied to our everyday life.

NOTE: In this week's lesson, I will make it easy for you to locate the answers to the six inductive study questions by providing their location within Scripture. As we move forward in our study of God's Word, you will learn to discover their location on your own.

1. Write Philippians 4:13 on the lines below.

_____

_____

_____

Now, let's address the Who, What, When, Where, Why, and How questions of Philippians 4:13.

2. Who is speaking? Who is being spoken to? **HINT:** You can discover these answers by reading the beginning of Paul's letter in Philippians 1:1.

_____

_____

3. What is Paul talking about? **HINT:** You can discover this answer by reading verses that surround Philippians 4:13. I recommend reading all of chapter 4.

_____

_____

_____

4. When is Paul writing? Where is he writing from? **HINT:** You can discover these answers by reading Philippians 1:7-20.

_____

_____

_____

NOTE: While we cannot discern the exact date or location of Paul's writing for this particular Scripture, we can get a general idea of the period in Paul's life and the place from which he is writing.

If you find yourself growing curious and desire to learn more about the people and places you're reading about, this would be a great time to pick up a reputable Bible commentary or New Testament introduction to discover the historical background of the text. In the appendix, I have included a list of recommended resources you may consider adding to your library for this very purpose.

There will be times, like this, when it's more difficult to answer one or more of the Observation questions. And, there will be times when knowing a specific answer to an Observation question does not necessarily impact our ability to put a passage of Scripture in its proper historical context. Therefore, if an answer is too hard to find and you don't have a reputable resource handy to help you in the process, feel free to skip the question and move on.

5. Why is the event or conversation taking place? **HINT:** You can discover this answer by reading Philippians 1:9-10, 12.

_____

_____

_____

To answer the question, "How is the conversation taking place?" we must consider the language of the book of Philippians and its historical background—the facts that support the truth Paul is communicating by means of a letter to the people of Philippi. As you begin to study more of God's Word, you'll find a great many of the "books" in the New Testament are actually "letters" written by the Apostles to the people they cared about.

Step 3: INTERPRET GOD'S WORD

What does the text mean? This important step focuses on determining the meaning of a passage. Unless we accurately determine the meaning of God's Word, we may inaccurately apply it to our life. Therefore, this step is one we must consider carefully.

By answering the Who, What, When, Where, Why, and How questions and by considering how Philippians 4:13 fits within its surrounding passages, we have worked to place this verse in its proper inductive context. Now, it's time to discover the Timeless Life Lesson(s) this verse provides.

NOTE: In most cases, there will be at least one Timeless Life Lesson in each verse or passage of Scripture you study. Sometimes there will be more than one. Each time you study a verse or passage, strive to identify at least one Timeless Life Lesson you can apply to your daily life.

1. In consideration of what you have observed and learned, what Timeless Life Lesson(s) do you believe God is trying to teach us in Philippians 4:13?

_____

_____

_____

_____

2. Has your understanding of Philippians 4:13 changed since your initial observation on day 1? If so, explain.

_____

_____

_____

_____

Step 4: APPLY GOD'S WORD

1. What do you need to do? This final, critical step allows God's Word to transform, if and only if we choose to employ it. Head knowledge that doesn't lead to heart change is futile.

2. How will you specifically apply these lessons to your life?

_____

_____

_____

_____

3. Journal additional thoughts God has placed on your heart regarding today's topic.

_____

_____

_____

_____

_____

_____

_____

_____

4. Write a prayer to God.

_____

_____

_____

_____

_____

_____

_____

_____

_____

_____

_____

Day FOUR: Establishing Best Practices

Practice this week's Courage Verse, John 8:31b-32. Now, try to recite it entirely from memory without glancing at your card. How did you do?

Today, let's further reinforce the habit of approaching God's Word inductively by continuing to practice the Four Basic Bible Study Steps. Today we will study James 2:14, 17.

Step 1: PRAY AS YOU APPROACH GOD'S WORD

1. Begin by asking the Holy Spirit to guide you into all truth. Take a few minutes and write a prayer thanking God for His Word. Ask Him to give you wisdom and discernment as you seek comfort and guidance through the study of Scripture.

_____

_____

_____

_____

Step 2: OBSERVE GOD'S WORD

1. Write James 2:14, 17 on the lines below.

_____

_____

_____

_____

What does the text say? To answer this question, it's time once again for the Who, What, When, Where, Why, and How questions of James 2:14, 17.

2. Who is speaking? Who is being spoken to? **HINT:** You can discover these answers by reading the beginning of this letter in James 1:1.

_____

_____

NOTE: If you are interested in learning more about James and his audience, pick up your favorite reputable commentary or New Testament introduction. You can explore his historical background and discover fascinating facts about the people to whom he wrote. If you choose to consult a commentary or introduction, describe your findings below.

_____

_____

_____

_____

3. What is James talking about? **HINT:** You can discover this answer by reading the verses that surround James 2:14, 17. I recommend reading all of chapter 2.

_____

_____

4. When is James writing? Where is he writing from?

NOTE: Although we cannot locate an exact date or location for the book of James in Scripture, we can research this information in our favorite, reputable commentary or New Testament introduction in which scholars provide a summary of the information they have uncovered through their research of Scripture and historical documents from that period. If you choose to consult a commentary or introduction, describe your findings below. Otherwise, feel free to skip this question since it doesn't necessarily have a bearing on our ability to discern the Timeless Life Lesson.

_____

_____

5. Why is the event or conversation taking place? **HINT:** You can discover this answer by reading the first chapter in the book of James.

_____

_____

_____

6. How is the conversation taking place?

NOTE: To answer this question, we must consider the language of the book of James and the historical background (just as we did with Philippians 4:13). By doing so, we can accurately answer this question:

James is communicating by means of a letter to the Jews who have been dispersed throughout the nations.

Step 3: INTERPRET GOD'S WORD

What does the text mean? Now that we have observed this verse in its proper inductive context by answering the Who, What, When, Where, Why, and How questions and by considering how the verse fits within surrounding passages and the book of James as a whole, it's time to discover the Timeless Life Lesson(s) it provides.

1. In consideration of what you have observed and learned, what Timeless Life Lesson(s) do you believe God is trying to teach us in James 2:14,17?

_____

_____

_____

_____

2. Has your understanding of James 2:14,17 changed since your initial observation on day 1? If so, Explain.

_____

_____

_____

_____

Step 4: APPLY GOD'S WORD

1. What do you need to do? How will you specifically apply this lesson(s) to your life?

_____

_____

_____

_____

2. Journal additional thoughts God has placed on your heart regarding today's topic.

_____

_____

_____

_____

_____

_____

_____

3. Write a prayer to God.

_____

_____

_____

_____

_____

_____

_____

Day FIVE: Tying It All Together

This is the final day of lesson 1. Can you recite this week's Courage Verse, John 8:31b-32, without looking at your card? If so, give yourself a high five!

Today, let's firmly establish the habit of approaching God's Word inductively by practicing the Four Basic Bible Study Steps for the third day in a row. Today we will study Acts 5:29.

Step 1: PRAY AS YOU APPROACH GOD'S WORD

1. Begin by asking the Holy Spirit to guide you into all truth. Take a few minutes and write a prayer thanking God for His Word. Ask Him to give you wisdom and discernment as you seek comfort and guidance through the study of Scripture.

_____

_____

_____

_____

Step 2: OBSERVE GOD'S WORD

1. Write Acts 5:29 on the lines below.

    _____

    _____

    _____

    Answer the Who, What, When, Where, Why, and How questions of Acts 5:29.

2. Who is speaking? Who is being spoken to? **HINT:** You can discover the answers by reading Acts 5:26-29.

    _____

    _____

    NOTE: Remember, we can also discover additional historical details about those speaking and their audience by consulting our favorite, reputable commentary or New Testament introduction.

3. What are the apostles talking about? **HINT:** You can discover this answer by reading Acts 5:17-32.

    _____

    _____

    _____

4. When were the apostles speaking? Where were they speaking from? **HINT:** You can discover these answers by reading Acts 1:1-8, 12; 2:1-4; 4:5-12; 5:16, 28.

    _____

    _____

    NOTE: This is another event for which we cannot locate a specific date, but once again, we can get a general timeframe and location by reading the surrounding passages or by referencing our favorite Bible commentary or New Testament introduction.

    When I first studied my Bible inductively, it was a bit of a challenge to develop this new perspective—then something miraculous happened. After practice, practice, and more practice, I found myself instinctively asking the Who, What, When, Where, Why, and How questions, and as I dug deeper, I discovered the incredible value of owning reputable Bible commentaries and New Testament and Old Testament introductions. The ability to discover additional historical details became fascinating and brought the Bible to life in a way I'd never imagined.

5. Why is the event or conversation taking place? **HINT:** You can discover this answer by reviewing Acts 1:1-8.

    _____

    _____

6. How is the conversation taking place? **HINT:** You can discover this answer by reading Acts 5:27.

_____

_____

_____

_____

Step 3: INTERPRET GOD'S WORD

Once again, we've observed today's verse in its proper inductive context by answering the Who, What, When, Where, Why, and How questions and by considering how it fits within the surrounding passages and the book of Acts as a whole. Now, it's time to discover the Timeless Life Lesson(s) contained within this passage.

1. What does the text mean? In consideration of what you have observed and learned, what Timeless Life Lesson(s) do you believe God is teaching us in Acts 5:29?

_____

_____

_____

_____

2. Has your understanding of Acts 5:29 changed since your initial observation on day 1? If so, explain.

_____

_____

_____

_____

Step 4: APPLY GOD'S WORD

1. What do you need to do? How will you specifically apply this lesson(s) to your life?

_____

_____

_____

_____

Now that we have learned and practiced the Four Basic Bible Study Steps, we have established a reliable foundation upon which we can build our steps to courage. Throughout the next eleven weeks, we will continue to exercise our inductive Bible study skills and discover truth from God's Word that will build our courage muscles and challenge our outlook for the future.

2. Journal additional thoughts God has placed on your heart regarding today's topic.

_____

_____

_____

_____

_____

_____

_____

3. Write a prayer to God. Ask Him to guide you through your journey to courage and to prepare your heart for courageous changes.

_____

_____

_____

_____

_____

_____

_____

_____

Congratulations! You've made it through this first critical week and completed lesson 1. You are well on your way to becoming a seasoned inductive student of the Bible. You've memorized your first Courage Verse and prepared yourself to journey toward courageous changes.

This week's lesson was all about readying our minds for the task at hand. We learned the Four Basic Bible Study Steps (P-O-I-A) that will enable us to approach God's Word with courage and confidence. We also established a firm foundation of biblical truth that will help us embrace our God-given courage to pursue our God-given dreams.

As we move on to lesson 2, "Find Courage," let's review and apply our Courage Quote, Courage Verse, and the Timeless Life Lessons from this week's study. By continuing in God's Word, we will know the truth, and the truth will make us free (John 8:32)!

LESSON 1

REVIEW

COURAGE QUOTE

God's Word transforms, but only to the depth we engage it and the pace at which we apply it.

COURAGE VERSE

If you continue in My word, then you are truly disciples of Mine; and you will know the truth, and the truth will make you free.

John 8:31b-32

Timeless Life Lessons Learned

_____

_____

_____

_____

_____

_____

_____

_____

_____

_____

_____

_____

FIND COURAGE

To face life with unwavering courage, we must first recognize its source: Christ.

Have I not commanded you? Be strong and courageous! Do not tremble or be dismayed, for the Lord your God is with you wherever you go.

–Joshua 1:9

Last week, we prepared for our twelve weeks together by learning the importance of approaching God's Word inductively. In addition, we learned and practiced the Four Basic Bible Study Steps that will aid us in discerning truth from God's Word. This week, we continue our journey toward courage by reading chapters 1 and 2, "Find Courage" and "Let Go of Fear," in our *CFL* book and by studying key passages in our Bible.

Day ONE: Defining "Courage"

Write this week's Courage Verse on a note card. Place it where you will see it often and practice memorizing it throughout the day. Read the introduction and chapter 1, "Find Courage," in your *CFL* book.

On pages 23 and 24 in *CFL*, I define "courage" with a list of definitions. Consider this list prayerfully. Ask God to give you the strength to admit your weaknesses as you identify the areas in which you struggle the most.

1. On the following lines, record your answers and include one to two sentences describing why you believe you struggle in these areas.

_____

_____

_____

_____

_____

_____

_____

_____

Complete Action Steps 1 and 2 of chapter 1 in CFL on page 27. Feel free to use a separate notebook or journal for the Action Step exercises or use the space provided below, along with the additional journal pages located in the appendix of this study guide.

2. Action Step 1: Jot down thoughts, tips, and Scripture notes from today's reading assignment.

_____

_____

_____

_____

_____

_____

3. Action Step 2: List the areas in your life where you might need to make more courageous choices.

_____

_____

_____

_____

_____

_____

4. Journal additional thoughts God has placed on your heart regarding today's topic.

_____

_____

_____

_____

_____

_____

5. Write a prayer to God.

_____

_____

_____

_____

_____

_____

_____

Day TWO: Identifying the Need for Courage

Begin today's study by practicing this week's Courage Verse, Joshua 1:9.

Read chapter 2 in *CFL,* "Let Go of Fear," and complete Action Steps 1 and 2 of chapter 2 on page 36.

1. Action Step 1: Take a courage/fear self-inventory by completing the chart below. In the appropriate column, list the ways you exhibit courage and/or fear—without judging your thoughts as right or wrong. Remember: The greatest enemy of courage is fear. The greatest conqueror of fear is faith.

COURAGE	FEAR

2. Action Step 2: Spend quiet time with the Lord, confessing relationships in your life where you struggle to forgive—including your relationship with yourself. Then ask God to help you as you begin to courageously embrace forgiveness in these relationships. Journal your thoughts here.

_____

_____

_____

_____

_____

_____

3. Journal additional thoughts God has placed on your heart regarding today's topics.

_____

_____

_____

_____

_____

_____

4. Write a prayer to God.

_____

_____

_____

_____

_____

Day THREE: Revealing the Enemy of Courage

Practice this week's Courage Verse, Joshua 1:9. Are you able to recite it without looking at your card? Try it and see.

Now let's study a key passage in God's Word that will shed light on the reality of courage and fear. Read the account of Elijah's challenge at Mount Carmel in 1 Kings 18:17-46, implement the Four Basic Bible Study Steps, and record your responses and findings. (If you need to refresh your memory about the details of each step, refer back to days 2 and 3 of lesson 1.)

Step 1: PRAY

1. Begin by asking the Holy Spirit to guide you into all truth. Take a few minutes and write a prayer thanking God for His Word. Ask Him to give you wisdom and discernment as you seek comfort and guidance through the study of Scripture.

_____

_____

_____

_____

Step 2: OBSERVE

What does this text say? In lesson 1, we observed Philippians 4:13; James 2:14, 17; and Acts 5:29 by asking specific Who, What, When, Where, Why, and How questions to place the verses in their proper context. In that first lesson, I provided "hints" by suggesting verses to assist you in finding the answers.

The passages we've studied so far were selected from letters and conversations; therefore, the questions we've asked have specifically related to written and verbal communication. As we move forward and observe other verses and passages of the Bible, we must adapt our questions, based on the type of conversation or event taking place in the text.

Therefore, beginning in this lesson—and throughout the remainder of this study—we will generalize our Who, What, When, Where, Why, and How questions, establishing effective questioning habits applicable to any passage of Scripture.

Answer as many of the Who, What, When, Where, Why, and How questions as you can, using 1 Kings 18:17-46 and its surrounding passages. Once you have answered the observations using Scripture, feel free to consult your favorite commentary or Old Testament introduction.

1 Kings 18:17-46

1. Who is speaking and being spoken to? Who is participating in the event? _____

_____

2. What is happening? What is being said? _____

_____

3. When is the event or conversation taking place? _____

_____

4. Where is the event or conversation taking place? _____

_____

5. Why is the event or conversation taking place? _____

_____

6. How is the event or conversation taking place? _____

_____

Step 3: INTERPRET

1. What does this text mean? What Timeless Life Lesson(s) do you believe God is trying to teach us?

_____

_____

_____

_____

_____

2. Briefly describe your perception of Elijah's courage.

_____

_____

_____

_____

_____

Step 4: APPLY

1. What do you need to do? How will you specifically apply this lesson(s) to your life?

_____

_____

_____

_____

_____

Read the account of Elijah's predicament in 1 Kings 19:1-4, implement the Four Basic Bible Study Steps, and record your responses and findings.

Step 1: PRAY

1. Begin by asking the Holy Spirit to guide you into all truth. Take a few minutes and write a prayer thanking God for His Word. Ask Him to give you wisdom and discernment as you seek comfort and guidance through the study of Scripture.

_____

_____

_____

_____

Step 2: OBSERVE

1 Kings 19:1-4

1. Who is speaking and being spoken to? Who is participating in the event? _____

_____

2. What is happening? What is being said? _____

_____

3. When is the event or conversation taking place? _____

_____

4. Where is the event or conversation taking place? _____

_____

5. Why is the event or conversation taking place? _____

_____

6. How is the event or conversation taking place? _____

_____

Step 3: INTERPRET

1. What does this text mean? What Timeless Life Lesson(s) do you believe God is trying to teach?

_____

_____

_____

_____

2. Briefly describe why you believe Elijah lost his courage.

_____

_____

_____

_____

_____

3. Can you relate to Elijah?

_____

_____

_____

Step 4: APPLY

1. What do you need to do? How will you specifically apply this lesson(s) to your life?

_____

_____

_____

_____

2. Journal additional thoughts God has placed on your heart regarding today's topic.

_____

_____

_____

_____

_____

_____

_____

3. Write a prayer to God.

_____

_____

_____

_____

_____

Day FOUR: Finding Courage

Practice this week's Courage Verse, Joshua 1:9. Now try to recite it entirely from memory without glancing at your card. How did you do?

Read the account of Esther in Esther 2:1 through 4:17, implement the Four Basic Bible Study Steps, and record your responses and findings.

Step 1: PRAY

1. Begin by asking the Holy Spirit to guide you into all truth. Take a few minutes and write a prayer thanking God for His Word. Ask Him to give you wisdom and discernment as you seek comfort and guidance through the study of Scripture.

_____

_____

_____

_____

_____

Step 2: OBSERVE

Esther 2:1-4:17

*Once you have answered the observation questions using Scripture, feel free to consult your favorite commentary or Old Testament introduction.

1. Who is speaking and being spoken to? Who is participating in the event?_____

_____

2. What is happening? What is being said?_____

_____

3. When is the event or conversation taking place?_____

_____

4. Where is the event or conversation taking place? _____

_____

5. Why is the event or conversation taking place? _____

_____

6. How is the event or conversation taking place? _____

_____

7. Briefly describe Esther's predicament and decision to choose courage.

_____

_____

_____

_____

8. What request did Esther make of Mordecai, the Jews, and her maidens? Could this request have prepared Esther with the courage she needed to approach King Ahasuerus? Explain.

_____

_____

_____

_____

Step 3: INTERPRET

1. What does this text mean? What Timeless Life Lesson(s) do you believe God is trying to teach us?

_____

_____

_____

_____

Step 4: APPLY

1. What do you need to do? How will you specifically apply this lesson(s) to your life?

_____

_____

_____

_____

2. Journal additional thoughts God has placed on your heart regarding today's topic.

_____

_____

_____

_____

3. Write a prayer to God.

_____

_____

_____

_____

_____

_____

Day FIVE: Recognizing the Provider of Courage

This is the final day of lesson 2. Can you recite this week's Courage Verse, Joshua 1:9, without looking at your card? If so, give yourself a high five!

During our time together, the last thing I want to do is bog you down with homework and hinder you from genuinely reflecting on each Timeless Life Lesson. Remember, the objective of completing this study is to apply what we learn to our daily lives so we can implement courageous changes. We want to complete this journey having gained God-given courage and confidence that will support us throughout the rest of our lives.

Throughout the next eleven weeks, I will ask you to consider several verses or passages of Scripture that pertain to specific topics. Since it is imperative we always consider each verse or passage in its proper context (but the Observation step in Bible study is often time consuming), I will occasionally provide you with the answers to the six observation questions as this will expedite your study process.

Today we are going to look at five key passages that help us recognize our ultimate source of courage. I have provided you with the observation information for Deuteronomy 31:6, Psalm 27:14, 1 Corinthians 10:13, Ephesians 6:10-18, and 2 Timothy 1:7 to expedite your study process and give you more time for reflection.

Write out these five passages, implement the Four Basic Bible Study Steps for each one, and record your responses and findings.

NOTE: As discussed in lesson 1, there will be times when a specific answer to an Observation question is not easy to discover and does not necessarily impact our ability to put the passage of Scripture in its proper historical context. Therefore, when providing answers to Observation questions in this lesson, and future lessons, I will occasionally note answers as "N/A" (Not Applicable) when this type of situation occurs.

Deuteronomy 31:6

_____

_____

_____

Psalm 27:14

_____

_____

_____

1 Corinthians 10:13

_____

_____

_____

Ephesians 6:10-18

_____

_____

_____

2 Timothy 1:7

_____

_____

_____

Step 1: PRAY

1. Begin by asking the Holy Spirit to guide you into all truth. Take a few minutes and write a prayer thanking God for His Word. Ask Him to give you wisdom and discernment as you seek comfort and guidance through the study of Scripture.

_____

_____

_____

_____

Step 2: OBSERVE

Deuteronomy 31:6

1. Who is speaking and being spoken to? Who is participating in the event?

   Moses is speaking to the people of Israel (Deut. 31:1).

2. What is happening? What is being said?

   Moses is giving his farewell speech to the people of Israel.[2]

3. When is the event or conversation taking place?

After Moses communicated God's commands, laws, and warnings to the people of Israel, but just before Joshua's commissioning, Moses's death, and the entry of Israel into the Land of Canaan. (Deut. 31:12-34).

4. Where is the event or conversation taking place?

In the plains of Moab, just north of the Dead Sea and east of the Jordan River, the staging area for the Israelites, just before they invaded the Land of Canaan (Deut. 29:1; 32:49).[3]

5. Why is the event or conversation taking place?

God promised to give the Israelites success as they entered the Promised Land. Therefore, Moses was reminding the people of Israel to be strong and unafraid when taking over the Land of Canaan.[4]

6. How is the event or conversation taking place?

Moses is personally addressing the assembly of Israel in Moab (Deut. 29:1).

Psalm 27:14

1. Who is speaking and being spoken to? Who is participating in the event?

This psalm is attributed to David and is, like all psalms, believed to be a spoken prayer to God.[5]

2. What is happening? What is being said?

David is making a plea to God and expressing his complete confidence that God will protect and deliver him.[6]

3. When is the event or conversation taking place?

N/A

4. Where is the event or conversation taking place?

N/A

5. Why is the event or conversation taking place?

David is praying for divine help and guidance.

6. How is the event or conversation taking place?

N/A

1 Corinthians 10:13

1. Who is speaking and being spoken to? Who is participating in the event?

Paul, an Apostle of Christ, is speaking to the church in Corinth (1 Cor. 1:1-2).

---

[2] Eugene Merrill, Mark F. Rooker, and Michael A. Grisanti, *The World and The Word: An Introduction to the Old Testament*, (Nashville: B&H Publishing Group, 2011), 259.

[3] Geoffrey W. Bromiley, ed., *The International Standard Bible Encyclopedia, Revised* (Grand Rapids, MI: Wm. B. Eerdmans, 1988), 881.

[4] Eugene H. Merrill, *The New American Commentary: Deuteronomy*, Vol. 4. (Nashville: Broadman & Holman Publishers, 1994), 397.

[5] Gerald H. Wilson, *The NIV Application Commentary: Psalms*. Vol. 1. (Grand Rapids, MI: Zondervan, 2002), 23, 89.

[6] Ibid., 482.

2. What is happening? What is being said?

   Paul is responding to the condition of the church and answering questions he received in a letter from the Corinthians.[7]

3. When is the event or conversation taking place?

   During Paul's third missionary journey.[8]

4. Where is the event or conversation taking place?

   Paul is believed to be in Ephesus when writing this letter. The church of Corinth was located in the city of Corinth, within the province of Achaia in Southern Greece.[9]

5. Why is the event or conversation taking place?

   Paul had received news that there was trouble in the church of Corinth. Evidently there was disunity within the church. Some of its members were practicing sexual immorality, and many were confused about marriage, sexual relationships, and gender roles.[10]

6. How is the event or conversation taking place?

   According to the structure of the book of Corinthians and its historical background, we can conclude Paul is communicating with the church of Corinth by letter.

Ephesians 6:10-18

1. Who is speaking and being spoken to? Who is participating in the event?

   Paul, an Apostle of Christ, is speaking to Gentile believers in Ephesus (Eph. 1:1; 3:1).

2. What is happening? What is being said?

   Paul is discussing the importance of unity within the church; he also addresses Christian ethics and spiritual warfare.[11]

3. When is the event or conversation taking place?

   Most likely, this letter was written while Paul was imprisoned (Eph. 6:20), sometime around AD 60.[12]

4. Where is the event or conversation taking place?

   The book of Ephesians is considered a Prison Epistle (a letter written by Paul when he was in prison); most scholars believe Paul likely wrote this letter during his imprisonment in Rome.[13]

5. Why is the event or conversation taking place?

   This is a general letter to the Ephesians to help believers understand the importance of living their lives as a reflection of their relationship with Christ.[14]

---

[7] Andreas J. Kostenberger, L. Scott Kellum, and Charles L. Quarles, *The Cradle, The Cross, And Crown: An Introduction to the New Testament* (Nashville: B&H Academic, 2016), 551, 557.

[8] Ibid., 546.

[9] Ibid., 547-548.

[10] Ibid., 551.

[11] Andreas J. Kostenberger, L. Scott Kellum, and Charles L. Quarles, *The Cradle, The Cross, And Crown: An Introduction to the New Testament* (Nashville: B&H Academic, 2016), 666.

[12] Ibid., 664.

6. How is the event or conversation taking place?

    According to the structure of the book of Ephesians and its historical background, Paul is communicating with believers in Ephesus by letter.

2 Timothy 1:7

1. Who is speaking and being spoken to? Who is participating in the event?

    Paul, an Apostle of Christ, is speaking to Timothy, his true child in the faith (1 Tim. 1:1-2).

2. What is happening? What is being said?

    Paul desired to instruct Timothy on how believers are to conduct themselves (1 Tim. 3:15).

3. When is the event or conversation taking place?

    Most likely, Paul is writing this letter to Timothy after being released from his first Roman imprisonment, in approximately AD 60.[15]

4. Where is the event or conversation taking place?

    N/A

5. Why is the event or conversation taking place?

    Paul desired to teach Timothy how to deal with false teachers and wanted to provide advice on other matters pertaining to the church.[16]

6. How is the event or conversation taking place?

    Paul is communicating with Timothy by letter (1 Tim. 3:14-15).

Step 3: INTERPRET

1. What do these texts mean? What Timeless Life Lessons do you believe God is trying to teach us?

    Deuteronomy 31:6

    _____

    _____

    _____

    Psalm 27:14

    _____

    _____

    _____

---

[13] Ibid.

[14] Klyne Snodgrass, The NIV Application Commentary: *Ephesians* (Grand Rapids, MI: Zondervan, 1996), 44.

[15] Andreas J. Kostenberger, L. Scott Kellum, and Charles L. Quarles, *The Cradle, The Cross, And Crown: An Introduction to the New Testament* (Nashville: B&H Academic, 2016), 731.

[16] Ibid., 734.

1 Corinthians 10:13

_____

_____

_____

Ephesians 6:10-18

_____

_____

_____

2 Timothy 1:7

_____

_____

_____

Step 4: APPLY

1. What do you need to do? How will you specifically apply these lessons to your life?

_____

_____

_____

_____

2. Journal additional thoughts God has placed on your heart regarding today's topic.

_____

_____

_____

_____

_____

_____

_____

3. Write a prayer to God.

_____

_____

_____

_____

_____

_____

_____

Congratulations! You've completed lesson 2 and challenged yourself in the areas of courage and fear. You've considered areas of your life where you need to make more courageous choices, and you've studied biblical accounts of godly men and women who relied on the strength of their faith and trusted in God to supply the courage they needed to overcome their fears.

As we move into lesson 3, "Navigate toward Change," let's review and apply our Courage Quote, Courage Verse, and Timeless Life Lessons from this week's study. By acknowledging our source of courage and choosing to apply truth to our everyday life, we will overcome our fears and embrace our God-given abilities.

LESSON 2

REVIEW

COURAGE QUOTE

To face life with unwavering courage, we must first recognize its source: Christ.

COURAGE VERSE

Have I not commanded you? Be strong and courageous! Do not tremble or be dismayed, for the Lord your God is with you wherever you go.

–Joshua 1:9

Timeless Life Lessons Learned

_____

_____

_____

_____

_____

_____

_____

_____

_____

_____

_____

NAVIGATE TOWARD CHANGE

Change requires time, persistence, and a plan; begin today and watch your future unfold.

And do not be conformed to this world, but be transformed by the renewing of your mind, so that you may prove what the will of God is, that which is good and acceptable and perfect.
–Romans 12:2

Last week we began developing our foundation for courage and took a closer look at the primary enemy of courage: fear. This week we will position ourselves to begin making courageous changes by reading chapters 3 and 4, in *CFL*, "Navigate toward Change" and "Lay the Foundation for Change," and by discussing critical components of our overall health. As we study passages from the Bible this week, we will continue implementing our Four Basic Bible Study Steps. Pretty soon, these important P-O-I-A steps will become second nature, and you will automatically implement them every time you read and study God's Word.

Day ONE: Preparing for Change

Write this week's Courage Verse on a note card. Place it where you will see it often and practice memorizing it throughout the day.

Read chapter 3 in *CFL*, "Navigate toward Change." During today's lesson, as we prepare for change, we will strive to renew our minds by intentionally shifting our focus toward healthier values, thoughts, attitudes, and behaviors.

1. On the following lines, write any detrimental values, thoughts, attitudes, and behaviors you sense God is encouraging you to change.

_____

_____

Complete Action Step 1 of chapter 3 on page 42.

2. Action Step 1: Take a few minutes and consider the negative inner voices that cause you to doubt yourself. List the messages you struggle with the most. I discuss the inner voices that accuse, judge, and threaten us on pages 39 and 40 of *CFL*.

3. Now, take a look at the two lists in chapter 12 of *CFL*, "Recognize the Truth Trifecta," on pages 136 through 139. Review "The Top Twenty Worldly Lies We Believe" and "The Top Twenty Truths That Replace Worldly Lies." Does any of your self-talk resemble these top twenty lies? If so, refer to "The Top Twenty Truth's That Replace Worldly Lies" chart and list the corresponding truths that replace the lies found in your negative messages.

4. Journal additional thoughts God has placed on your heart regarding today's topic.

5. Write a prayer to God.

_____

_____

_____

_____

_____

_____

Day TWO: Identifying Boundaries

Practice this week's Courage Verse, Romans 12:2.

Throughout the Bible, God instructs us to set boundaries, which can help us avoid sin and suffering. Read Exodus 20:1-17, implement the Four Basic Bible Study Steps, and record your responses and findings.

Step 1: PRAY

1. Begin by asking the Holy Spirit to guide you into all truth. Take a few minutes and write a prayer thanking God for His Word.

_____

_____

_____

Step 2: OBSERVE

Exodus 20:1-17

1. Who is speaking and being spoken to? Who is participating in the event? _____

_____

2. What is happening? What is being said? _____

_____

3. When is the event or conversation taking place? _____

_____

4. Where is the event or conversation taking place? _____

_____

5. Why is the event or conversation taking place? _____

_____

6. How is the event or conversation taking place? _____

_____

Step 3: INTERPRET

1. What does this text mean? What Timeless Life Lesson(s) do you believe God is trying to teach us?

_____

_____

_____

_____

2. What boundary commands did you discover in this passage?

_____

_____

_____

_____

Step 4: APPLY

1. What do you need to do? How will you specifically apply this lesson(s) to your life?

_____

_____

_____

_____

2. Complete Action Step 2 of chapter 3, on page 42, by answering the following four questions.

    a. Write a few paragraphs about what healthy boundaries mean to you.

    _____

    _____

    _____

    _____

    _____

    _____

    _____

_____

_____

_____

_____

_____

_____

_____

_____

_____

b. Why do you believe it is important for us to set boundaries in our lives?

_____

_____

_____

_____

_____

_____

c. Can you think of some of the consequences we might face if we fail to establish boundaries in our lives?

_____

_____

_____

_____

_____

_____

d. List at least one boundary area you feel you need to change.

_____

_____

_____

_____

_____

_____

3. Journal additional thoughts God has placed on your heart regarding today's topic.

_____

_____

_____

_____

_____

_____

_____

_____

_____

4. Write a prayer to God.

_____

_____

_____

_____

_____

_____

_____

_____

_____

_____

_____

Day THREE: Analyzing Foundational Health

Practice this week's Courage Verse, Romans 12:2. Are you able to recite it without looking at your card? Try it and see.

Read chapter 4 in *CFL,* "Lay the Foundation for Change."

1. Using the chart on the next page, complete Action Step 1 of chapter 4, found on page 51 in *CFL*. On a scale of one to ten, rate your current health condition. Record your answers next to each abbreviated category on the chart. (If needed, refer back to the lists that demonstrate healthy traits of each of the Four Foundations of Health, on pages 45, 46, 48 and 49 in your *CFL* book, and review each category of health.)

NOTE: The goal of this assessment is to recognize areas of our health we desire to improve. It is not meant to discourage us. We *all* struggle in various areas of foundational health, and depending on our current life circumstances, some areas may be more of a struggle than others.

Spiritual Health	Emotional Health	Relational Health	Physical Health
Give and Receive Forgiveness	Recognize, Identify, Express, & Manage Feelings	Listen Non-judgmentally, Value Others, & Support Their Goals	Maintain Strength, Flexibility, & Endurance through Daily Activity
Articulate Your Salvation Experience	Build & Sustain Healthy Relationships	Respect, Accept, & Consider Others' Feelings, Opinions, Activities, & Interests	Follow a Balanced Diet
Recognize God's Presence & Power	Overcome Painful Experiences, Self-destructive Patterns, & Distorted Beliefs	Communicate Truth-in-Love	Abstain from Abuse of Drugs and Alcohol
Study & Apply Biblical Truth	Be Transparent about Needs and Feelings	Acknowledge & Accept Responsibility; Ask for Forgiveness When Wrong	Promptly Address Medical Conditions
Share & Defend the Gospel	Love, Respect, & Forgive in Spite of Differences	Face Conflict, Recognize Resolutions, Implement Solutions, & Communicate with Care	Rest and Relax Regularly
Pray, Worship, & Fellowship with Others	Continually Self-Examine Thoughts & Actions	Love, Respect, & Forgive in Spite of Differences	Honor Body as God's Temple
Daily Quiet Time of Praying & Listening to God	Face Conflict, Manage Emotions Positively, & Communicate Care	Receptive to & Understanding of Others' Needs & Feelings	Maintain Proper Water Intake

Complete Action Step 2 of chapter 4, found on page 52 in *CFL.*

2. Action Step 2: Write down your weakest areas of health. Pray for wisdom and discernment and ask God to tell you how you can strengthen these areas. Then describe ways you can improve your overall health.

_____

_____

_____

_____

_____

_____

3. Journal additional thoughts God has placed on your heart regarding today's topic.

_____

_____

_____

_____

_____

_____

4. Write a prayer to God.

_____

_____

_____

_____

_____

_____

Day FOUR: Discovering Truth for Spiritual and Emotional Health

Practice this week's Courage Verse, Romans 12:2. Now try to recite it entirely from memory without glancing at your card. How did you do?

Read Colossians 2:6-8, implement the Four Basic Bible Study Steps, and record your responses and findings. I have provided the Observation information to expedite your study process.

Step 1: PRAY

1. Begin by asking the Holy Spirit to guide you into all truth. Take a few minutes and write a prayer thanking God for His Word.

_____

_____

_____

Step 2: OBSERVE

Colossians 2:6-8

1. Who is speaking and being spoken to? Who is participating in the event?

   Paul, an apostle of Christ, (with Timothy) is speaking to faithful believers in Colossae (Col. 1:1-2).

2. What is happening? What is being said?

   Paul is speaking out against false teachers and warning believers to keep Christ the central focus of their lives.[17]

3. When is the event or conversation taking place?

   Paul is writing in approximately AD 60.[18]

4. Where is the event or conversation taking place?

   Paul is believed to have been writing from prison (Col. 4:10).

5. Why is the event or conversation taking place?

   Paul wants to oppose the false teachers and encourage believers to remain true to Christ.[19]

6. How is the event or conversation taking place?

   Paul is communicating with the Colossians by letter (Col. 4:16).

7. Summarize Paul's account of the components and purpose of Spiritual Health.

   _____

   _____

   _____

---

[17] Andreas J. Kostenberger, L. Scott Kellum, and Charles L. Quarles, *The Cradle, The Cross, And Crown: An Introduction to the New Testament* (Nashville: B&H Academic, 2016), 678-679.

[18] Ibid., 678.

[19] Frank E. Gaebelein, A. Skevington Wood, Homer A. Kent Jr., Curtis Vaugn, Robert L. Thomas, Ralph Earle, D. Edmond Hiebert, and Arthur A. Rupprecht. *The Expositor's Bible Commentary: Ephesians through Philemon*, Vol. 11 (Grand Rapids, MI: Zondervan Publishing House, 1981), 196.

Step 3: INTERPRET

1. What does this text mean? What Timeless Life Lesson(s) do you believe God is trying to teach us?

_____

_____

_____

_____

_____

Step 4: APPLY

1. What do you need to do? How will you specifically apply this lesson(s) to your life?

_____

_____

_____

2. Describe your Spiritual Health.

_____

_____

_____

3. Do you have any Spiritual Health goals? Share them here.

_____

_____

_____

4. What changes do you sense God encouraging you to make regarding your Spiritual Health?

_____

_____

_____

Read Galatians 5:16-24, implement the Four Basic Bible Study Steps, and record your responses and findings. I have provided the Observation information to expedite your study process.

Step 1: PRAY

1. Begin by asking the Holy Spirit to guide you into all truth. Take a few minutes and write a prayer thanking God for His Word.

_____

_____

_____

_____

Step 2: OBSERVE

Galatians 5:16-24

1. Who is speaking and being spoken to? Who is participating in the event?

    Paul, an Apostle of Christ, is speaking to the churches of Galatia (Gal. 1:1-2).

2. What is happening? What is being said?

    Paul makes his argument against salvation based on man's ability and efforts to keep God's law.[20]

3. When is the event or conversation taking place?

    Galatians was most likely written in AD 48-49.[21]

4. Where is the event or conversation taking place?

    _N/A_

5. Why is the event or conversation taking place?

    Soon after Paul left Galatia, false teachers made their way into the churches and began distorting the gospel by insisting believers must also keep the law of Moses.[22]

6. How is the event or conversation taking place?

    Paul is communicating with the Galatians by letter (Gal. 1:20).

7. Summarize what you've learned from this passage about our battle against the flesh and how this battle attacks our Emotional Health.

    _____

    _____

    _____

    _____

---

[20] Andreas J. Kostenberger, L. Scott Kellum, and Charles L. Quarles, _The Cradle, The Cross, And Crown: An Introduction to the New Testament_ (Nashville: B&H Academic, 2016), 483.

[21] Ibid., 494.

[22] Ibid., 495.

Step 3: INTERPRET

1. What does this text mean? What Timeless Life Lesson(s) do you believe God is trying to teach us?

Step 4: APPLY

1. What do you need to do? How will you specifically apply this lesson(s) to your life?

2. Describe the state of your current Emotional Health.

3. Do you have any Emotional Health goals? Share them here.

4. What changes do you sense God encouraging you to make regarding your Emotional Health?

5. Journal additional thoughts God has placed on your heart regarding today's topic.

_____

_____

_____

_____

_____

_____

6. Write a prayer to God.

_____

_____

_____

_____

_____

_____

_____

Day FIVE: Discovering Truth for Relational and Physical Health

This is the final day of lesson 3. Can you recite this week's Courage Verse, Romans 12:2, without looking at your card? If so, give yourself a high five!

Read Ephesians 4, implement the Four Basic Bible Study Steps, and record your responses and findings. I have provided the Observation information to expedite your study process.

Step 1: PRAY

1. Begin by asking the Holy Spirit to guide you into all truth. Take a few minutes and write a prayer thanking God for His Word.

_____

_____

_____

_____

Step 2: OBSERVE

Ephesians 4

1. Who is speaking and being spoken to? Who is participating in the event?

    Paul, an apostle of Christ, is speaking to Gentile believers in Ephesus (Eph. 1:1; 3:1).

2. What is happening? What is being said?

    Paul discusses the importance of unity within the church; he also addresses Christian ethics and spiritual warfare.[23]

3. When is the event or conversation taking place?

    Most likely, this letter was written while Paul was imprisoned (Eph. 6:20), sometime around AD 60.[24]

4. Where is the event or conversation taking place?

    Ephesians is considered a Prison Epistle; most scholars believe Paul likely wrote this letter during his imprisonment in Rome.[25]

5. Why is the event or conversation taking place?

    This is a general letter to the Ephesians to help believers understand the importance of our life with Christ.[26]

6. How is the event or conversation taking place?

    According to the structure of the book of Ephesians and its historical background, we can conclude Paul is communicating with believers in Ephesus by letter.

7. Summarize Paul's account of the components and purpose of healthy relationships.

    _____

    _____

    _____

    _____

Step 3: INTERPRET

1. What does this text mean? What Timeless Life Lesson(s) do you believe God is trying to teach us?

    _____

    _____

    _____

    _____

---

[23] Andreas J. Kostenberger,, L. Scott Kellum, and Charles L. Quarles, *The Cradle, The Cross, And Crown: An Introduction to the New Testament* (Nashville: B&H Academic, 2016), 666.

[24] Ibid., 664.

[25] Ibid.

[26] Klyne Snodgrass, *The NIV Application Commentary: Ephesians.* (Grand Rapids, MI: Zondervan, 1996), 44.

Step 4: APPLY

1. What do you need to do? How will you specifically apply this lesson(s) to your life?

2. Describe your Relational Health.

3. Do you have any Relational Health goals? Share them here.

4. What changes do you sense God encouraging you to make regarding your Relational Health?

Read the following passages on the importance of caring for our bodies, 1 Corinthians 6:19-20 and 3 John 1:2. Implement the Four Basic Bible Study Steps, and record your responses and findings. I have provided the Observation information to expedite your study process.

Step 1: PRAY

1. Begin by asking the Holy Spirit to guide you into all truth. Take a few minutes and write a prayer thanking God for His Word.

_____

_____

_____

_____

_____

_____

Step 2: OBSERVE

1 Corinthians 6:19-20

1. Who is speaking and being spoken to? Who is participating in the event?

    Paul, an Apostle of Christ, is speaking to the church in Corinth (1 Cor. 1:1-2).

2. What is happening? What is being said?

    Paul is responding to the condition of the church and answering the Corinthian's questions, which they presented to him in a letter.[27]

3. When is the event or conversation taking place?

    During Paul's third missionary journey (1 Cor. 16:8), in AD 53 or 54.[28]

4. Where is the event or conversation taking place?

    Paul is in Ephesus, and the church of Corinth was located in the city of Corinth, within the province of Achaia in Southern Greece.[29]

5. Why is the event or conversation taking place?

    Paul had received news that there was trouble in the church of Corinth. Evidently there was disunity within the church. Some of its members were practicing sexual immorality, and many were confused about marriage, sexual relationships, and gender roles.[30]

6. How is the event or conversation taking place?

    According to the structure of the book of Corinthians and its historical background, we can conclude Paul is communicating with the church of Corinth by letter.

---

[27]   Andreas J. Kostenberger, L. Scott Kellum, and Charles L. Quarles, *The Cradle, The Cross, And Crown: An Introduction to the New Testament* (Nashville: B&H Academic, 2016), 551 and 557.

[28]   Ibid., 546.

[29]   Ibid., 547-548.

[30]   Ibid., 551.

3 John 1:2

1. Who is speaking and being spoken to? Who is participating in the event?

    The Apostle John, son of Zebedee, is speaking to a believer named Gaius (3 Jn. 1).

2. What is happening? What is being said?

    John is writing to a dear friend (3 Jn. 1), in anticipation of his visit (3 Jn. 14), to address an issue with a particular church member.[31]

3. When is the event or conversation taking place?

    Early to mid-90s AD[32]

4. Where is the event or conversation taking place?

    N/A

5. Why is the event or conversation taking place?

    Paul writes to commend and encourage Gaius for his hospitality toward visiting missionaries (3 Jn. 5-8) and to inform him of his intention to confront Diotrephes personally regarding his evil deeds.[33]

6. How is the event or conversation taking place?

    John is writing to Gaius by means of a letter (3 Jn. 13-14).

7. Write a brief description of what you have learned from God's Word regarding the importance of caring for our physical bodies.

    _____

    _____

    _____

    _____

Step 3: INTERPRET

1. What do these texts mean? What Timeless Life Lesson(s) do you believe God is trying to teach us?

    1 Corinthians 6:19-20

    _____

    _____

    _____

---

[31] Gary M. Burge, *The NIV Application Commentary: Letters of John* (Grand Rapids, MI: Zondervan Publishing House, 1996), 245-248.

[32] Andreas J. Kostenberger, L. Scott Kellum, and Charles L. Quarles, *The Cradle, The Cross, And Crown: An Introduction to the New Testament* (Nashville: B&H Academic, 2016), 904.

[33] Gary M. Burge, *The NIV Application Commentary: Letters of John* (Grand Rapids, MI: Zondervan Publishing House, 1996), 245-246.

3 John 1:2

_____

_____

_____

Step 4: APPLY

1. What do you need to do? How will you specifically apply this lesson(s) to your life?

_____

_____

_____

_____

2. Describe your Physical Health.

_____

_____

_____

_____

3. Do you have any Physical Health goals? Share them here.

_____

_____

_____

_____

4. What changes do you sense God encouraging you to make regarding your Physical Health?

_____

_____

_____

_____

5. Write a few sentences describing how each of the Four Foundations of Health impact one another, in both positive and negative ways.

_____

_____

_____

_____

_____

_____

6. Journal additional thoughts God has placed on your heart regarding today's topic.

_____

_____

_____

_____

_____

7. Write a prayer to God.

_____

_____

_____

_____

_____

Congratulations! You've completed lesson 3, taken an inventory of your overall health, and discovered what God's Word has to say about the Four Foundations of Health.

As we move on to lesson 4, "Commit to Change," let's review and apply our Courage Quote, Courage Verse, and Timeless Life Lessons. By acknowledging weaknesses within our Spiritual, Emotional, Relational, and Physical Health, we are better prepared to identify areas that require courageous changes, a critical process as we navigate toward change.

LESSON 3

REVIEW

COURAGE QUOTE

Change requires time, persistence, and a plan; begin today and watch your future unfold.

COURAGE VERSE

And do not be conformed to this world, but be transformed by the renewing of your mind, so that you may prove what the will of God is, that which is good and acceptable and perfect.

–Romans 12:2

Timeless Life Lessons Learned

_____

_____

_____

_____

_____

_____

_____

_____

_____

_____

_____

C STEP IN COURAGE

COMMIT TO CHANGE

Commitments require courage to stay the course and reap the reward.

Brethren, I do not regard myself as having laid hold of it yet; but one thing I do:
forgetting what lies behind and reaching forward to what lies ahead,
I press on toward the goal for the prize of the upward call of God in Christ Jesus.

–Philippians 3:13-14

Now that we've discussed courage, fear, and change, our next lesson brings us to the heart of the message God placed in my spirit when I wrote the book *Courage For Life*. It represents the first step in our acronym of COURAGE, C = Commit to Change.

Last week, we navigated toward change by discussing healthy boundaries and laid the foundation for change by analyzing our overall health and studying Scripture. This week, we will focus on our commitment to make God-inspired, courageous changes by reading chapters 5 and 6, in our *CFL* book, "Commit to Change" and "Pinpoint the Change," and by studying Scripture that challenges us to follow through.

We will continue to implement and practice the Four Basic Bible Study Steps, and we will analyze what I call the ABCDs of Change, specific areas of our overall health in which we commonly struggle.

Day ONE: Commit to Change

Write this week's Courage Verse on a note card. Place it where you will see it often and practice memorizing it throughout the week.

Read pages 55 through 57 of chapter 5 in *CFL,* "Commit to Change" (stopping at the header "Attitude.")

1. In your own words, define the word "commitment."

_____

_____

_____

_____

2. Is it a struggle for you to follow through with your commitments? If so, why? Briefly describe your struggle.

_____

_____

_____

_____

Read Ruth 1:1-18, implement the Four Basic Bible Study Steps, and record your responses and findings.

Step 1: PRAY

1. Begin by asking the Holy Spirit to guide you into all truth. Take a few minutes and write a prayer thanking God for His Word.

_____

_____

_____

_____

Step 2: OBSERVE

Ruth 1:1-18

1. Who is speaking and being spoken to? Who is participating in the event?_____

_____

2. What is happening? What is being said?_____

_____

3. When is the event or conversation taking place? _____

_____

4. Where is the event or conversation taking place? _____

_____

5. Why is the event or conversation taking place?_____

_____

6. How is the event or conversation taking place? _____

_____

7. Write a few sentences to describe Ruth's commitment to Naomi.

_____

_____

_____

_____

8. How difficult might this commitment have been for Ruth and why?

_____

_____

_____

9. Compare Ruth 4:13-17 and Matthew 1:1-6 with Ruth 1:1-18. Briefly describe the blessing Ruth received as a result of her commitment.

NOTE: It's not always necessary to implement the Four Basic Bible Study Steps when comparing verse to verse, especially for this section of today's lesson, since we are primarily researching Ruth's descendants. But, any time you don't fully understand the meaning of a verse or passage, whether comparing verse to verse or studying a specific verse or passage on its own, you will always want to consider its context before determining the meaning and application.

_____

_____

_____

Step 3: INTERPRET

1. What does this text mean? What Timeless Life Lesson(s) do you believe God is trying to teach us?

_____

_____

_____

_____

2. Are there any areas in your life you sense God is encouraging you to make a commitment?

_____

_____

_____

_____

Step 4: APPLY

1. What do you need to do? How will you specifically apply this lesson(s) to your life?

2. Journal additional thoughts God has placed on your heart regarding today's topic.

3. Write a prayer to God.

Day TWO: Uncovering Strongholds

Before you begin today's study, practice this week's Courage Verse, Philippians 3:13-14. Next, read pages 57 through 60 of chapter 5 in *CFL* (stopping at the header "Behavior").

Read Philippians 2:1-18, implement the Four Basic Bible Study Steps, and record your responses and findings.

Step 1: PRAY

1. Begin by asking the Holy Spirit to guide you into all truth. Take a few minutes and write a prayer thanking God for His Word.

_____

_____

Step 2: OBSERVE

Philippians 2:1-18

1. Who is speaking and being spoken to? Who is participating in the event? _____

   _____

2. What is happening? What is being said? _____

   _____

3. When is the event or conversation taking place? _____

   _____

4. Where is the event or conversation taking place? _____

   _____

5. Why is the event or conversation taking place? _____

   _____

6. How is the event or conversation taking place? _____

   _____

7. In the following chart, by referring to Philippians 2:1-18, list the attitudes we are to adopt under the header "Believers." Then, list the attributes that describe Christ's attitude that we are to reflect, under the header "Christ."

Believers	Christ

Step 3: INTERPRET

1. What does this text mean? What Timeless Life Lesson(s) do you believe God is trying to teach us?

_____

_____

_____

Step 4: APPLY

1. What do you need to do? How will you specifically apply this lesson(s) to your life?

_____

_____

_____

_____

2. Journal additional thoughts God has placed on your heart regarding today's topic.

_____

_____

_____

_____

_____

_____

3. Write a prayer to God.

_____

_____

_____

_____

_____

_____

_____

Day THREE: Considering Behaviors and Beliefs

Practice this week's Courage Verse, Philippians 3:13-14. Are you able to recite it without looking at your card? Try it and see.

Read the remainder of chapter 5, pages 61 through 64 in *CFL* (beginning at the header "Behavior").

Read 2 Samuel 12:1-15, implement the Four Basic Bible Study Steps, and record your responses and findings. I have provided the Observation information to expedite your study process.

Step 1: PRAY

1. Begin by asking the Holy Spirit to guide you into all truth. Take a few minutes and write a prayer thanking God for His Word.

_____

_____

_____

_____

Step 2: OBSERVE

2 Samuel 12:1-15

1. Who is speaking and being spoken to? Who is participating in the event?

   The prophet Nathan and King David are having a conversation (2 Sam. 7:2; 12:1,7).

2. What is happening? What is being said?

   God sent Nathan to confront David about murdering Uriah and taking Uriah's wife to be his own (2 Sam. 12:1,9).

3. When is the event or conversation taking place?

   During King David's reign over Israel (2 Sam. 8:15-1; Kings 1:39).

4. Where is the event or conversation taking place?

   At King David's house (2 Sam. 11:27-12:1).

5. Why is the event or conversation taking place?

   Because King David had ignored God's Word and sinned against Him (2 Sam. 12:9).

6. How is the event or conversation taking place?

   Nathan confronts King David personally (2 Sam. 12:1).

7. Briefly describe the account of Nathan's confrontation with David.

   _____

   _____

   _____

   _____

8. What was David's response at the end of the passage?

   _____

   _____

   _____

   _____

Step 3: INTERPRET

1. What does this text mean? What Timeless Life Lesson(s) do you believe God is trying to teach us?

   _____

   _____

   _____

   _____

Read Psalm 32:1-5, implement the Four Basic Bible Study Steps, and record your responses and findings. I have provided you with the Observation information to expedite your study process.

Step 1: PRAY

1. Begin by asking the Holy Spirit to guide you into all truth. Take a few minutes and write a prayer thanking God for His Word.

_____

_____

_____

_____

Step 2: OBSERVE

Psalm 32:1-5

1. Who is speaking and being spoken to? Who is participating in the event?

    This psalm is attributed to David and is a spoken prayer of repentance and thanksgiving to God.[34]

2. What is happening? What is being said?

    King David is expressing sorrow for his sin and thankfulness for God's forgiveness (Ps. 32).

3. When is the event or conversation taking place?

    It is believed that this psalm was written in response to King David's sin, possibly his sin with Bathsheba. Therefore, this psalm was likely written during King David's reign.[35]

4. Where is the event or conversation taking place?

    _N/A_

5. Why is the event or conversation taking place?

    It is believed that this psalm was written in response to King David's sin, possibly his sin with Bathsheba.[36]

6. How is the event or conversation taking place?

    _N/A_

Step 3: INTERPRET

1. What does this text mean? What Timeless Life Lesson(s) do you believe God is trying to teach us?

    _____

    _____

    _____

    _____

---

[34] Frank E. Gaebelein, Willem VanGemern, Allen P. Ross, J. Stafford Wright, and Dennis F. Kinlaw, _The Expositor's Bible Commentary: Psalms, Proverbs, Ecclesiastes, Song of Songs_, Vol. 5 (Grand Rapids, MI: Zondervan Publishing House, 1991), 270.

[35] Ibid., 272-273.

[36] Ibid.

2. Now that we've studied both 2 Samuel 12:1-15 and Psalm 32:1-5, let's consider how these passages might apply to us. Describe the consequences we experience when we hide our sin versus the blessings we receive when we acknowledge, confess, and repent of our sin.

_____

_____

_____

_____

Step 4: APPLY

1. What do you need to do? How will you specifically apply this lesson(s) to your life?

_____

_____

_____

_____

Complete Action Steps 1 and 2 of chapter 5, found on page 64 in *CFL.*

2. Action Step 1: Review the chart, "Development of a Stronghold," on page 58. Then list any strongholds you are aware of in your life.

_____

_____

_____

_____

_____

3. Action Step 2: List any specific attitudes or behaviors you feel led to commit to change. Include areas of change God brought to your attention as you read chapter 5 and worked through this lesson.

_____

_____

_____

_____

_____

_____

4. Journal additional thoughts God has placed on your heart regarding today's topic.

_____

_____

_____

_____

_____

_____

5. Write a prayer to God.

_____

_____

_____

_____

_____

_____

_____

_____

Day FOUR: Recognizing Circumstances and Coping Skills

Practice this week's Courage Verse, Philippians 3:13-14. Now try to recite it entirely from memory without glancing at your card. Are you getting better at doing this?

Read pages 65 through 70 of chapter 6 in *CFL*, "Pinpoint the Change" (ending at the header "Defining Our Desires" on page 70).

Read Genesis 37:1-4, 18-28, implement the Four Basic Bible Study Steps, and record your responses and findings.

Step 1: PRAY

1. Begin by asking the Holy Spirit to guide you into all truth. Take a few minutes and write a prayer thanking God for His Word.

_____

_____

_____

_____

Step 2: OBSERVE

Genesis 37:1-4, 18-28

1. Who is speaking and being spoken to? Who is participating in the event? _____
   _____

2. What is happening? What is being said? _____
   _____

3. When is the event or conversation taking place? _____
   _____

4. Where is the event or conversation taking place? _____
   _____

5. Why is the event or conversation taking place? _____
   _____

6. How is the event or conversation taking place? _____
   _____

Read Genesis 42:1-8, 45:1-8, and 50:20, implement the Four Basic Bible Study Steps, and record your responses and findings.

Step 1: PRAY

1. Begin by asking the Holy Spirit to guide you into all truth. Take a few minutes and write a prayer thanking God for His Word.

_____

_____

_____

_____

_____

Step 2: OBSERVE

Genesis 42:1-8, 45:1-8, and 50:20

1. Who is speaking and being spoken to? Who is participating in the event? _____
   _____

2. What is happening? What is being said? _____
   _____

3. When is the event or conversation taking place? _____

_____

4. Where is the event or conversation taking place? _____

_____

5. Why is the event or conversation taking place? _____

_____

6. How is the event or conversation taking place? _____

_____

Read Genesis 39:1, 6-10, implement the Four Basic Bible Study Steps, and record your responses and findings.

Step 1: PRAY

1. Begin by asking the Holy Spirit to guide you into all truth. Take a few minutes and write a prayer thanking God for His Word.

_____

_____

_____

_____

Step 2: OBSERVE

Genesis 39:1, 6-10

1. Who is speaking and being spoken to? Who is participating in the event? _____

_____

2. What is happening? What is being said? _____

_____

3. When is the event or conversation taking place? _____

_____

4. Where is the event or conversation taking place? _____

_____

5. Why is the event or conversation taking place? _____

_____

6. How is the event or conversation taking place? _____

_____

7. Briefly describe how Joseph responded to and coped with the various circumstances he encountered throughout his life.

_____

_____

_____

_____

_____

Step 3: INTERPRET

1. What do these three texts from Genesis mean? What Timeless Life Lesson(s) do you believe God is trying to teach us?

_____

_____

_____

_____

_____

2. Are there circumstances in your life that you can (and perhaps need to) change?

_____

_____

_____

_____

3. Are there difficult circumstances in your life you are truly unable to change? If so, why?

_____

_____

_____

_____

4. Does your perspective or attitude toward any of the circumstances you listed need to change?

_____

_____

_____

_____

Step 4: APPLY

1. What do you need to do? How will you specifically apply these lessons from Genesis to your life?

_____

_____

_____

_____

2. Journal additional thoughts God has placed on your heart regarding today's topic.

_____

_____

_____

_____

_____

_____

_____

3. Write a prayer to God.

_____

_____

_____

_____

_____

_____

_____

Day FIVE: Defining Our Desires

This is the final day of lesson 4. Can you recite this week's Courage Verse, Philippians 3:13-14, without looking at your card? If so, applaud your success!

Read the remainder of chapter 6 in *CFL*, "Pinpoint the Change," (beginning at the header "Defining Our Desires" on page 70).

Now read 1 Peter 1:13-16, implement the Four Basic Bible Study Steps, and record your responses and findings. I have provided the Observation information to expedite your study process.

Step 1: PRAY

1. Begin by asking the Holy Spirit to guide you into all truth. Take a few minutes and write a prayer thanking God for His Word.

_____

_____

_____

_____

Step 2: OBSERVE

1 Peter 1:13-16

1. Who is speaking and being spoken to? Who is participating in the event?

   Peter, an Apostle of Christ, is speaking to believers throughout Asia Minor: Pontus, Galatia, Cappadocia, Asia, and Bithynia (1 Pet. 1:1).

2. What is happening? What is being said?

   Peter is encouraging Christians to endure persecution.[37]

3. When is the event or conversation taking place?

   Approximately AD 62-63.[38]

4. Where is the event or conversation taking place?

   The letter was sent from Babylon (1 Pet. 5:13) to believers throughout Pontus, Galatia, Cappadocia, Asia, and Bithynia (1 Pet. 1:1).

5. Why is the event or conversation taking place?

   Because believers were suffering and needed encouragement (1 Pet. 1:6-8; 2:19-21; 3:16-17; 4:4-7,12-14, 19).

6. How is the event or conversation taking place?

   Peter is communicating with believers by letter (1 Pet. 5:12).

Step 3: INTERPRET

1. What does this text mean? What Timeless Life Lesson(s) do you believe God is trying to teach us?

_____

_____

_____

_____

---

[37] Andreas J. Kostenberger, L. Scott Kellum, and Charles L. Quarles, _The Cradle, The Cross, And Crown: An Introduction to the New Testament_ (Nashville: B&H Academic, 2016), 840-841.

[38] Ibid., 839.

Step 4: APPLY

1. What do you need to do? How will you specifically apply this lesson(s) to your life?

    _____

    _____

    _____

    _____

    Complete Action Steps 1 and 2 of chapter 6, found on pages 71 and 72 in *CFL*.

2. Action Step 1: List any specific circumstances, coping skills, or desires you feel led to change. Include additional areas of change God brought to your attention as you read chapter 6.

    _____

    _____

    _____

    _____

    _____

    _____

3. Action Step 2: Ask God to help you sincerely commit to change (see Joshua 1:9, Romans 12:2). Consider sharing your insights with a trusted friend who will encourage, support, and hold you accountable as you prepare to make necessary changes. Describe your commitment.

    _____

    _____

    _____

    _____

    _____

    _____

4. Action Step 2: Our study this week has been focused on the *C* Step to COURAGE, Commit to Change. As we look back over the past four days, identify the top three commitments you desire to make over the next eight weeks.

    1. _____

    _____

    2. _____

    _____

    3. _____

    _____

5. Journal additional thoughts God has placed on your heart regarding today's topic.

_____

_____

_____

_____

_____

_____

_____

6. Write a prayer to God.

_____

_____

_____

_____

_____

_____

_____

_____

Congratulations! You've completed lesson 4 and have studied specific passages that inspire courageous commitment and changes in your attitudes, behaviors, beliefs, circumstances, coping skills, and desires.

As we move on to lesson 5, "Overcome Obstacles," let's review and apply our Courage Quote, Courage Verse, and Timeless Life Lessons from this week's study. By acknowledging and making commitments to change areas of our lives, we take our first major step in our journey to courage.

LESSON 4

REVIEW

Commitments require courage to stay the course and reap the reward.

Brethren, I do not regard myself as having laid hold of it yet; but one thing I do:
forgetting what lies behind and reaching forward to what lies ahead,
I press on toward the goal for the prize of the upward call of God in Christ Jesus.

–Philippians 3:13-14

Timeless Life Lessons Learned

_____

_____

_____

_____

_____

_____

_____

_____

_____

_____

0 STEP IN COURAGE

OVERCOME OBSTACLES

To unleash our God-given courage, we must dismantle our exasperating obstacles.

I can do all things through Him who strengthens me.

–Philippians 4:13

Obstacles hinder progress. They seek to hold us hostage and deter us from fully embracing our God-given potential. Last week, we listed three primary commitments to change God is prompting us to make. To begin making these changes, we must overcome obstructions that hinder us from taking necessary steps forward. This week, we will diligently work to identify and break down these pesky roadblocks. We will read chapters 7 and 8, "Overcome Obstacles" and "Ten Common Obstacles," in our *CFL* book and review Scripture that challenges us to overcome obstacles standing in the way of our courageous progress.

Day ONE: Exposing Underlying Pests

Write this week's Courage Verse on a note card. Place it where you will see it often and practice memorizing it throughout the week. As we begin to identify our obstacles, let's take a close look at four primary issues that are often at their root.

Read chapter 7 in *CFL,* "Overcome Obstacles." Now, let's review the Four Pests of Pressure and consider how each of these pests personally impacts our everyday life decisions.

The Four Pests of Pressure

P.O.P. #1: *Fear*

Fear is a devastating pest that can eat away at our lives. While fear sometimes manifests as a necessary warning or caution, it can also be a mighty deterrent in areas of life we need to embrace more freely. Today, we are going to consider unnecessary fears that create inappropriate roadblocks. I love what Franklin D. Roosevelt said about overcoming our fears: "Courage is not the absence of fear, but rather the assessment that something else is more important than fear."

1. Review the list of common fears on pages 79 and 80 in *CFL* and describe which of these fears challenge you the most.

_____

_____

_____

_____

2. Are there any additional fears, not listed on pages 79 and 80 of *CFL*, that commonly hinder you from courageously pursuing your commitment and calling or from making necessary life changes?

_____

_____

_____

_____

3. Write 2 Timothy 1:7 below and be reminded of God's promise regarding fear.

_____

_____

_____

_____

P.O.P. #2: *Hurt*

Hurt is a debilitating pest that can hold our hearts captive.

1. Describe any past or present hurts that chip away at your ability to courageously move forward in true freedom.

_____

_____

_____

2. Write Hebrews 12:15 below and be reminded of our need to allow God's grace to heal our hurt and free us from bitterness and other emotional hindrances.

_____

_____

_____

P.O.P. #3: *Sin*

Sin is a powerfully destructive pest that seeks to overpower our desires and ultimately destroy our lives. On page 81 in *CFL*, I describe three types of sin we are exposed to each and every day.

1. List and describe these three types of sin.

    1. _____

       _____

    2. _____

       _____

    3. _____

       _____

2. Can you identify one or more specific sins that negatively influence your daily decisions, desires, behaviors, actions, and relationships?

    _____

    _____

    _____

    _____

    _____

3. Write 1 Corinthians 10:13 below and be reminded we are not alone in our struggle with sin. Embrace God's sovereign promises found in this verse and rest assured we *can* overcome our temptation to sin when we rely on God's presence, provisions, and power.

    _____

    _____

    _____

P.O.P. #4: *Shame*

Shame is a detestable pest that can undermine every aspect of our Spiritual, Emotional, Relational, and Physical Health. On page 83 in *CFL*, I include a paragraph from *Daring Greatly* by Brene' Brown. These few words pack a powerful punch.

1. What do you think about this paragraph? Write a few sentences to describe how you define "shame."

    _____

    _____

    _____

    _____

2. Are you aware of any areas in your life where shame threatens to undermine your courage, confidence, and overall health?

    _____

    _____

    _____

3. Write Micah 7:19 below and be reminded of how God overcame our sin and set us free, once-and-for-all, from shame and self-condemnation.

    _____

    _____

    _____

4. Journal additional thoughts God has placed on your heart regarding today's topic.

    _____

    _____

    _____

    _____

    _____

    _____

5. Write a prayer to God.

    _____

    _____

    _____

    _____

    _____

    _____

Day TWO: Confronting Common Obstacles

To begin our study today, practice this week's Courage Verse, Philippians 4:13.

Over the next four days, we are going to confront the Top Ten Common Obstacles that deter many of us from making positive, courageous changes. Some of us intensely struggle with these obstacles, while others find them merely aggravating. No matter the level of intensity, we must honestly assess each obstacle and put practical and proven strategies in place to begin overcoming them.

Read pages 85 through 89 of chapter 8 in *CFL*, "Ten Common Obstacles," (ending at the header "Expectations").

The Bible has much to say about each of these Top Ten Common Obstacles. For this lesson, instead of incorporating our Four Basic Bible Study Steps, I will list several passages that encourage us to confront and overcome these pesky roadblocks. For the following exercises, read and meditate on each passage, ask God for guidance, and allow the Holy Spirit to prompt your responses to each question.

Common Obstacle #1: Relational Conflicts

Applicable passages for review: Romans 12:17-21; Matthew 18:15-17; Luke 17:3; Colossians 3:12-14

Realizing not all relational conflict can be resolved, list one or more relationships God is encouraging you to work on. Journal your contribution to any conflict within the relationship and your willingness to forgive and/or ask for forgiveness. List at least one positive action you will take this week to move toward repairing each relationship.

_____

_____

_____

_____

_____

_____

_____

_____

_____

_____

Remember, we are only responsible for following through with actions God is encouraging us to take. We are not responsible for the responses of those we are reaching out to. Once we have followed through with our positive contribution toward reconciliation, we must let go, release the relationship completely to God, and rejoice over our willingness to overcome this obstacle.

Common Obstacle #2: Codependency

Applicable passages for review: Galatians 1:10, 6:1; 1 Thessalonians 2:4; Proverbs 29:15

1. On pages 87 through 89 in *CFL,* with the help of several experts, I describe and define "codependency." After reviewing these pages, how would you define codependency?

_____

_____

_____

_____

2. Are you aware of any codependent traits you struggle with that keep you from pursuing courageous choices and changes? If so, explain.

_____

_____

_____

_____

3. If you struggle with codependent traits, reread the last paragraph in *CFL's* section on codependency on pages 88 and 89, write a plan of action to address this obstacle, and take positive steps to overcome this crippling condition.

_____

_____

_____

_____

Common Obstacle #3: Triggers and Landmines

Applicable passages for review: Romans 8:5-6, 12:2; Colossians 3:2; Proverbs 25:28

1. On page 89 in *CFL,* I discuss emotional triggers and landmines. After reviewing this page, describe how you define "triggers" and "landmines."

Triggers:

_____

_____

_____

Landmines:

_____

_____

_____

2. Can you identify any emotional triggers or landmines you struggle with that provoke you to overreact? If so, describe each one.

_____

_____

_____

_____

_____

_____

Identifying triggers and landmines is the first step in overcoming them. Once we've identified a trigger or landmine, it's important we share our struggle with a safe friend or loved one. By bringing our struggles into the open and discussing them, we become more acutely aware of their existence and will begin to *appropriately act* rather than *inappropriately overreact.*

On pages 92 and 93 in *CFL,* I discuss the importance of finding and having safe friends who will listen attentively, love unconditionally, and offer godly advice without judgment. Throughout this study, I will often recommend you reach out to a safe friend or loved one. This will be one of the most important components of your healing process. Just as we learned from our study of King David on day 3 last week, sin—especially done in isolation—only complicates our problems. To overcome and fully heal, we must bring our issues into the light among safe friends, loved ones, and/or a Christian counselor.

3. Write a plan of action, one that includes communication with safe friends and loved ones, that will help you appropriately act when these triggers and/or landmines occur.

_____

_____

_____

_____

_____

_____

4. Journal additional thoughts God has placed on your heart regarding today's topic.

_____

_____

_____

_____

_____

_____

5. Write a prayer to God.

_____

_____

_____

_____

_____

_____

Day THREE: Confronting Common Obstacles

Practice this week's Courage Verse, Philippians 4:13. Are you able to recite it without looking at your card? Try it and see.

Now, let's confront three more of our Top Ten Common Obstacles: expectations, anger, and isolation. Again, read each applicable passage, ask God for guidance, and allow the Holy Spirit to prompt your responses.

Read pages 90 through 93 of chapter 8 in _CFL_, "Ten Common Obstacles," (beginning at the header "Expectations" and ending at the header "Anxiety and Stress").

Common Obstacle #4: Expectations

Applicable passages for review: Philippians 4:6, 19; Galatians 6:9; Romans 12:12

Our expectations can be a real obstacle, especially if they are unrealistic or unreasonable. Expectations fall into one of three categories: completely appropriate, completely unreasonable, or somewhere in between. It's up to us to make an honest assessment of our expectations and identify the unreasonable ones that hinder us from making informed, helpful, and courageous decisions.

1. Identify your unmet expectations and describe them below. Beside each unmet expectation, place the letter "A" if you believe the expectation is appropriate or "U" if God is convicting you to admit it's unrealistic or unreasonable. If you are unsure, or feel your unmet expectation lies somewhere in-between, put a question mark by its description.

    _____

    _____

    _____

    _____

    _____

2. Write out a prayer to God below, surrendering your realistic and unrealistic expectations to Him. Release them completely and rejoice over your willingness to overcome this obstacle.

    _____

    _____

    _____

    _____

_____

_____

Common Obstacle #5: Anger

Applicable passages for review: Proverbs 14:29; Ephesians 4:26; James 1:19-20; Ecclesiastes 7:9

Anger is a common emotion that often arises when we struggle with one or more of our Pests of Pressure. Once we identify the root cause of our anger, we can begin working to manage and even overcome it.

1. What makes you angry? Come on; don't hold back. Write it all down.

_____

_____

_____

_____

_____

_____

2. Do you outwardly express your anger toward others or allow it to build up internally, causing anxiety, stress, sleeplessness, and worry? Explain.

_____

_____

_____

_____

_____

_____

3. Can you identify the underlying issue(s) fueling your anger? Briefly describe the circumstances you believe are igniting your emotions and try to identify one or more of the Pests of Pressure (fear, hurt, sin, or shame) that may be contributing to your anger.

_____

_____

_____

_____

_____

4. Describe ways you believe God is encouraging you to cope, manage, or overcome your anger.

_____

_____

_____

_____

_____

_____

Common Obstacle #6: Isolation and Secrecy

Applicable passages for review: Ecclesiastes 4:9-10; Proverbs 18:1, 27:17; James 5:16

The enemy loves to isolate us. Just as a bully on the playground will isolate a vulnerable child, our enemy attempts to isolate us and convince us that we will be rejected if we transparently share our struggles, needs, and dreams with others.

Once we accept that isolation is our enemy and not a place of safety, we can begin to break down the walls that keep us in hiding. We can then learn to share our struggles with others in safe environments, and we can ultimately heal.

1. Do you isolate or hide your fear, hurt, sin, or shame from others? Do you fear exposure, judgment, or a fallout if you open up? Briefly explain.

_____

_____

_____

_____

2. In what ways do you sense God encouraging you to come out of isolation? Can you name at least one or two safe friends or loved ones with whom you are willing to share your deepest, darkest secrets? Write a commitment and action plan to overcome isolation.

_____

_____

_____

_____

3. Journal additional thoughts God has placed on your heart regarding today's topic.

_____

_____

_____

_____

_____

_____

4. Write a prayer to God.

_____

_____

_____

_____

_____

_____

Day FOUR: Confronting Common Obstacles

Practice this week's Courage Verse, Philippians 4:13. Now, try to recite it entirely from memory without glancing at your card. How did you do?

Today we will confront three more of our Top Ten Common Obstacles: anxiety, un-forgiveness, and addiction. Again, read each applicable passage, ask God for guidance, and allow the Holy Spirit to prompt your responses.

Read pages 93 through 95 of chapter 8 in *CFL*, "Ten Common Obstacles" (beginning at the header "Anxiety and Stress" and ending at the header "Addictions").

Common Obstacle #7: Anxiety and Stress

Applicable passages for review: Proverbs 12:25; John 14:27; Matthew 6:27; Ecclesiastes 4:6

Anxiety and stress can permeate every area of our lives: personal, relational, and professional. It's another tool Satan uses to separate us from God's promise to never leave us or forsake us (Heb. 13:5).

1. What areas of your life produce anxiety and stress and prevent you from a life of contentment and joy?

_____

_____

_____

_____

_____

_____

_____

2. Pray and ask God to reveal ways in which you can reduce the amount of anxiety and stress in your life. What commitments are you willing to make to lower your stress levels?

_____

_____

_____

_____

_____

_____

_____

Common Obstacle #8: Bitterness and Unforgiveness

Applicable passages for review: Mark 12:31; Matthew 6:14-15; Ephesians 4:31-32; Luke 6:37

God's Word encourages us to forgive those who have hurt us. Jesus, being the greatest model of forgiveness, hung on the cross and prayed passionately for his persecutors: "Father, forgive them; for they do not know what they are doing" (cf. Lk. 23:34).

1. Are bitterness and unforgiveness crippling your relationships and sabotaging other parts of your life? Name those you need to forgive, even if it includes yourself, and describe your willingness to forgive.

_____

_____

_____

_____

_____

_____

_____

2. Do you sense God encouraging you to overcome bitterness and unforgiveness? Write a commitment and action plan to overcome this obstacle.

_____

_____

_____

_____

_____

Common Obstacle #9: Addiction

Applicable passages for review: 2 Peter 2:19; 1 Corinthians 10:13; Hebrews 4:15-16; Philippians 4:13

Addictions are crippling. They can be chemical and/or behavioral and are simply anything we engage in habitually to escape our reality.

1. Are there any addictions you need to overcome? Ask God to give you the courage to identify them. Write an honest assessment of your struggle and desire to overcome addiction. Facing your addiction may be one of the hardest things you'll ever do—but the results will be worth it.

_____

_____

_____

_____

_____

Addictions are *not* always something we can overcome alone. Are you willing to reach out for help? Yesterday, I asked you to name at least one or two safe friends or loved ones you are willing to share your deepest, darkest secrets with. Pray and ask God to give you the courage to confess your addiction to your safe friend or loved one. Ask her to pray for you and support you as you seek help. If you were unable to identify a safe friend or loved one, find a local support group or counselor through Celebrate Recovery, The American Association of Christian Counselors, Narcotics Anonymous, or Alcoholics Anonymous.

2. Write your commitment to get help and follow through by reaching out for support.

_____

_____

_____

_____

_____

3. Journal additional thoughts God has placed on your heart regarding addiction.

_____

_____

_____

_____

_____

4. Write a prayer to God.

_____

_____

_____

_____

_____

_____

_____

Day FIVE: Confronting Common Obstacles

This is the final day of lesson 5. Can you recite this week's Courage Verse, Philippians 4:13, without looking at your card? If so, bravo!

Today, we come to our fourth and final day confronting our top Ten Common Obstacles. As we close out this week's lesson, we will tackle a topic that, in one way or another, impacts practically all of us: abuse. Just as you've done for the past three days, read each applicable passage, ask God for guidance, and allow the Holy Spirit to prompt your responses.

Read the remainder of chapter 8 in *CFL*, "Ten Common Obstacles," on pages 95 through 99 (beginning at the header "Addictions").

Common Obstacle #10: Abuse

Applicable passages for review: Psalm 91; Isaiah 61:1-3; Jeremiah 15:19-21; Matthew 18:15-17

Abuse has many facets and degrees. Consider these staggering statistics:

- "On average, nearly 20 people per minute are physically abused by an intimate partner in the United States. During one year, this equates to more than 10 million women and men."[39]
- "1 in 3 women and 1 in 4 men have been victims of [some form of] physical violence by an intimate partner within their lifetime."[40]

1. After today's reading, what is your understanding of God's view of abuse?

_____

_____

_____

_____

_____

2. Review the list on page 98 in *CFL* titled, "Healthy Relationship vs. Abusive Relationship." Are you personally experiencing any abusive behaviors listed under the Abusive Relationship column? If so, explain. Remember, no one is looking at your notes—this is your opportunity to unload any burden you carry.

_____

_____

_____

_____

_____

3. Are you exhibiting any abusive behaviors listed under the Abusive Relationship column? If so, explain.

_____

_____

_____

_____

_____

4. Do you know anyone personally who is experiencing or exhibiting abusive behaviors? If so, explain.

_____

_____

_____

_____

_____

Abuse is a very serious offense. It is emotionally, and often physically, destructive to the victim and requires an immediate, carefully thought-out response. Like addiction, it often cannot be dealt with alone.

5. If you or someone you know is the victim of abuse, write a commitment to seek appropriate help in addressing the situation.

_____

_____

---

[39] National Coalition Against Domestic Abuse, http://ncadv.org/learn-more/statistics, accessed September 1, 2016.

[40] Ibid.

_____

_____

6. If you or someone you know exhibits abusive behavior, write a commitment to seek help in establishing appropriate boundaries and to share your knowledge of this behavior with at least one or two safe friends or loved ones and/or a qualified counselor.

_____

_____

_____

We have covered many difficult topics this week. Take the next ten to fifteen minutes to reflect on the obstacles you have uncovered. Ask God to help you digest everything you have learned in this lesson.

Complete Action Steps 1 and 2 of chapter 8 on page 99 in _CFL_.

7. Action Step 1: After reading chapters 7 and 8, have you identified any additional obstacles that negatively impact your foundational health? List any additional obstacles you need to overcome.

_____

_____

_____

_____

_____

_____

Listen attentively to God and ask Him for guidance as you strive to overcome these obstacles. Then reach out to a safe person, admit your obstacles, and ask for support as you work to conquer them. Don't wait. Get help.

8. Action Step 2: Beside each obstacle you listed, list one or more of the Four Pests of Pressure contributing to your struggle: fear, hurt, sin, and/or shame. Remember, there may be more than one of these culprits underpinning each obstacle.

As we've worked through this difficult step in COURAGE, I've repeatedly mentioned the need to share our struggles with safe friends and loved ones. I want to encourage you once more to reach out and share your hurt, frustration, and fears. Remember, the enemy of our soul will continue to encourage us to isolate, but God is calling us to come out of hiding. He is waiting and willing to give us the courage we need to take this step.

9. Write your commitment to ask for help as you work through the challenging process of overcoming your obstacles.

_____

_____

10. Journal additional thoughts God has placed on your heart regarding today's topic.

_____

_____

_____

_____

_____

_____

11. Write a prayer to God.

_____

_____

_____

_____

_____

_____

I understand, this particular lesson may have been hard on you, but I want to congratulate you for hanging in there and working through it. You've successfully completed lesson 5 and taken inventory of the Four Pests of Pressure that seek to hold you hostage. You also bravely confronted the Top Ten Common Obstacles that seek to hinder you on your journey toward courageous change.

Now that we've worked through the first two COURAGE steps, we have prepared ourselves for the next essential step: the _U_ Step to COURAGE, Uncover Your True Self.

As we move on to lesson 6, "Uncover Your True Self," let's review and apply our Courage Quote, Courage Verse, and Timeless Life Lessons from this week's study and allow God to strengthen us in all things He has called us to do.

LESSON 5

REVIEW

COURAGE QUOTE

To unleash our God-given courage, we must dismantle our exasperating obstacles.

COURAGE VERSE

I can do all things through Him who strengthens me.

–Philippians 4:13

Timeless Life Lessons Learned

_____

_____

_____

_____

_____

_____

_____

_____

_____

_____

U STEP IN COURAGE

UNCOVER YOUR TRUE SELF

To embrace life in true freedom, we must embrace ourselves with complete acceptance.

I will give thanks to You, for I am fearfully and wonderfully made;
Wonderful are Your works, and my soul knows it very well.

–Psalm 139:14

O ver the past few weeks, we've worked to establish our foundation for courageous change. We've grounded our journey in God's Word, made commitments to implement necessary changes, and identified ways to overcome our obstacles. This week we will focus on fully embracing how God sees us. Thus, we will learn to place how others see us—and how we see ourselves—in proper perspective.

Day ONE: Embracing Truth

Write this week's Courage Verse on a note card. Place it where you will see it often and practice memorizing it throughout the week.

Read chapter 9 in *CFL,* "Uncover Your True Self."

1. Briefly describe how you see yourself, your strengths, weaknesses, gifts, and areas of difficulty.

_____

_____

_____

_____

_____

2. Are there parts of your true identity you tend to cover up? If so, explain why you feel the need to hide your *true self* from others.

_____

_____

_____

_____

_____

3. Review the list of Scripture references at the bottom of page 108 and top of page 109 of chapter 9 in *CFL*. Based on these verses, describe your understanding of how God sees you.

_____

_____

_____

_____

_____

_____

Complete Action Steps 1 and 2 of chapter 9 on page 110 in *CFL*.

4. Action Step 1: Take out four note cards and write the following verses on each one: Psalm 139:14 and Ephesians 2:10. Place these cards where you will see them frequently throughout your day and read them repeatedly until you have memorized each.

5. Action Step 2: Take an honest assessment of your view of yourself. Is your view mostly positive or negative? Are you willing to adopt God's view over yours? Explain your answers to these questions here.

_____

_____

_____

_____

_____

6. Journal additional thoughts God has placed on your heart regarding today's topic.

_____

_____

_____

_____

_____

_____

7. Write a prayer to God.

_____

_____

_____

_____

_____

_____

Day TWO: Exploring God-Given Needs and Feelings

Practice this week's Courage Verse, Psalm 139:14. Read pages 111 through 119 of chapter 10 in *CFL*, "Unmask Your Authentic Identity" (ending at the header "Exchange False Masks for True Identity").

1. Review the three common reasons we cover up, on pages 112 and 114 of chapter 10 in *CFL*, and record which reason(s) best describes why you tend to hide parts of your true self from others.

_____

_____

_____

_____

_____

2. Our view of ourselves is often impacted by our understanding of our needs. Review the five God-given needs mentioned on page 116 of chapter 10 in *CFL* and describe which of these needs commonly go unmet in your life.

_____

_____

_____

_____

_____

3. List the unmet needs you identified, pray over each one, and ask God to reveal ways He would like to meet your needs. Beside each need, write at least one change you sense God encouraging you to make that will help meet your God-given needs.

_____

_____

_____

_____

_____

Beginning on page 117 of chapter 10 in *CFL*, I discuss the importance of understanding our primary (underlying) and secondary (surface) feelings. Being able to recognize the difference between the two is extremely valuable and takes practice.

4. Review the list "Surface Feelings vs. Underlying Feelings" on page 118 in *CFL*. List the surface feelings you commonly experience and try to identify the underlying feeling or feelings that are likely fueling each surface feeling.

_____

_____

_____

_____

_____

5. Today we've discussed the importance of appropriately communicating our God-given needs and feelings. Now, take an honest assessment and describe your ability to effectively and appropriately communicate your needs and feelings with safe friends and loved ones.

_____

_____

_____

_____

_____

I discussed isolation quite a bit in lesson 5. But, having first-hand experience of how challenging it can be to break this habit, I believe it bears additional encouragement. If sharing needs and feelings with others is still a struggle for you, ask God once again to reveal at least one or two appropriate, safe people who will offer you the opportunity to exercise transparency.

Remember, not everyone is comfortable receiving hard or troubling disclosures. Therefore, we must allow God to direct us to those who will lovingly listen, validate our needs and feelings, and offer godly encouragement and accountability. The best, safest friendships are those wherein *each* person shares transparently, listens compassionately, and maintains confidentiality. When searching for a safe friendship, be sure you offer to be a safe friend in return.

6. Write down the name or names God reveals, along with your commitment to meet with them as regularly as possible to practice sharing your God-given needs and feelings.

_____

_____

_____

_____

_____

_____

_____

7. Journal additional thoughts God has placed on your heart regarding today's topic.

_____

_____

_____

_____

_____

_____

_____

_____

8. Pray for the courage to embrace transparency and vulnerability around a few safe friends. Write a prayer to God.

_____

_____

_____

_____

_____

_____

Day THREE: Managing Emotions

Practice this week's Courage Verse, Psalm 139:14. Are you able to recite it without looking at your card?

God gave us our feelings and emotions as warning signals to help us know when something in our lives needs to be examined. He uses our emotions to draw us closer to Him and move us in the direction of His will for our lives.

Throughout the Gospels, we see the depth of Christ's emotions. Toward the Pharisees, temple merchants, and money changers, Christ expressed righteous anger (Mk. 3:5; 11:15); regarding the destruction of Israel, the betrayal of one friend and the death of another, Christ expressed intense grief (Lk. 19:41, 22:21-22,44; Jn. 11:33-36); toward the leper, the outcast, and the lame and suffering, Christ expressed compassion (Mk. 1:40-41; Matt. 9:36, 20:33-34; Lk. 7:13). And regarding the loyalty of His followers and God's great mercy and promise for our future, Christ expressed great joy (Jn. 15:11, 17:13; Lk. 10:21).

As we pursue spiritual growth, in our journey to become more like Christ, we must strive to model His ways of managing emotions. Let's learn more about God's expectations for maintaining control over difficult emotions. Today we will explore how we are to manage anger and grief.

Managing Anger

Read Ephesians 4:26-27, implement the Four Basic Bible Study Steps, and record your responses and findings.

We studied Ephesians chapter 4 in lesson 3, day 5. Answer the Observation questions for Ephesians 4:26-27 by reviewing the information provided to you in lesson 3.

Step 1: PRAY

1. Begin by asking the Holy Spirit to guide you into all truth. Take a few minutes and write a prayer thanking God for His Word.

Step 2: OBSERVE

Ephesians 4:26-27

1. Who is speaking and being spoken to? Who is participating in the event?

2. What is happening? What is being said?

3. When is the event or conversation taking place? _____
   _____

4. Where is the event or conversation taking place? _____
   _____

5. Why is the event or conversation taking place? _____
   _____

6. How is the event or conversation taking place? _____
   _____

Step 3: INTERPRET

1. What does this text mean? What Timeless Life Lesson(s) do you believe God is trying to teach us?

   _____
   _____
   _____
   _____

2. Briefly describe your understanding of our responsibility to manage our anger.

   _____
   _____
   _____
   _____

Step 4: APPLY

1. What do you need to do? How will you specifically apply this lesson(s) to your life?

   _____
   _____
   _____
   _____

Managing Grief

Read Matthew 14:1-14, implement the Four Basic Bible Study Steps, and record your responses and findings. I have provided the Observation information to expedite your study process.

Step 1: PRAY

1. Begin by asking the Holy Spirit to guide you into all truth. Take a few minutes and write a prayer thanking God for His Word.

    _____

    _____

    _____

    _____

Step 2: OBSERVE

Matthew 14:1-14

1. Who is speaking and being spoken to? Who is participating in the event?

    Matthew, an apostle of Christ and eyewitness to the life of Christ, is recording this historical account for believers.[41]

2. What is happening? What is being said?

    Matthew is writing about Herod's concern that Jesus is John the Baptist reincarnated, and he describes the account of John the Baptist's execution (Matt. 14:10).

3. When is the event or conversation taking place?

    John the Baptist was beheaded during the reign of Herod Antipas (Matt. 14:1), during Jesus' ministry (Matt. 14:12-13). Matthew wrote this account sometime prior to the destruction of Jerusalem in AD 70.[42]

4. Where is the event or conversation taking place?

    Jesus was in his hometown, Nazareth (Matt. 13:54), when he heard about John the Baptist's death. He then "withdrew from there in a boat to a secluded place" (Matt. 14:13).

5. Why is the event or conversation taking place?

    The death of John the Baptist took place because of Herodias's jealousy and hatred of him (Matt. 14:3-8).

6. How is the event or conversation taking place?

    N/A

7. Briefly describe the circumstances that led to Christ's grief. Note how He expressed His grief and how He responded toward the people who followed Him.

    _____

    _____

    _____

    _____

---

[41] Andreas J. Kostenberger, L. Scott Kellum, and Charles L. Quarles, *The Cradle, The Cross, And Crown: An Introduction to the New Testament* (Nashville: B&H Academic, 2016), 226.

[42] Ibid., 232.

Step 3: INTERPRET

1. What does this text mean? What Timeless Life Lesson(s) do you believe God is trying to teach us?

Step 4: APPLY

1. What do you need to do? How will you specifically apply this lesson(s) to your life?

2. Journal additional thoughts God has placed on your heart regarding today's topic.

3. Write a prayer to God.

Day FOUR: Embracing Emotions

Practice this week's Courage Verse, Psalm 139:14. Now try to recite it entirely from memory without glancing at your card. How did you do? As you have memorized this verse, have you become more accepting of the fact you are fearfully and wonderfully made by God?

Yesterday, we discussed how we must manage challenging or difficult emotions, and we analyzed what the Bible says about two such emotions, anger and grief. Today, we will explore our need to fully embrace positive emotions, like compassion and joy.

Managing Compassion

Read Colossians 3:12-14, implement the Four Basic Bible Study Steps, and record your responses and findings. I have provided the Observation information to expedite your study process.

Step 1: PRAY

1. Begin by asking the Holy Spirit to guide you into all truth. Take a few minutes and write a prayer thanking God for His Word.

_____

_____

_____

_____

Step 2: OBSERVE

Colossians 3:12-14

1. Who is speaking and being spoken to? Who is participating in the event?

   Paul, an apostle of Christ, (with Timothy) is speaking to faithful believers in Colossae (Col. 1:1-2).

2. What is happening? What is being said?

   Paul is speaking out against false teachers and warning believers to keep Christ the central focus of their lives.[43]

3. When is the event or conversation taking place?

   Paul is writing in approximately AD 60.[44]

4. Where is the event or conversation taking place?

   Paul is believed to have been writing from prison (Col. 4:10).

5. Why is the event or conversation taking place?

   Paul wants to oppose the false teachers and encourage believers to remain true to Christ.[45]

---

[43] Andreas J. Kostenberger, L. Scott Kellum, and Charles L. Quarles, *The Cradle, The Cross, And Crown: An Introduction to the New Testament* (Nashville: B&H Academic, 2016), 678-679.

6. How is the event or conversation taking place?

Paul is communicating with the Colossians by means of a letter (Col. 4:16).

Step 3: INTERPRET

1. What does this text mean? What Timeless Life Lesson(s) do you believe God is trying to teach us?

_____

_____

_____

_____

2. Briefly describe your understanding of our responsibility to have and openly express compassion.

_____

_____

_____

_____

Step 4: APPLY

1. What do you need to do? How will you specifically apply this lesson(s) to your life?

_____

_____

_____

_____

Managing Joy

Read Romans 15:13, implement the Four Basic Bible Study Steps, and record your responses and findings. I have provided the Observation information to expedite your study process.

---

44 Ibid., 678.

45 Frank E. Gaebelein, A. Skevington Wood, Homer A. Kent Jr., Curtis Vaugn, Robert L. Thomas, Ralph Earle, D. Edmond Hiebert, and Arthur A. Rupprecht. *The Expositor's Bible Commentary: Ephesians through Philemon.* Vol. 11 (Grand Rapids, MI: Zondervan Publishing House, 1981), 196.

Step 1: PRAY

1. Begin by asking the Holy Spirit to guide you into all truth. Take a few minutes and write a prayer thanking God for His Word.

_____

_____

_____

_____

Step 2: OBSERVE

Romans 15:13

1. Who is speaking and being spoken to? Who is participating in the event?

   Paul, an apostle of Christ, is speaking to Christians who lived in Rome (Rom. 1:7).

2. What is happening? What is being said?

   Paul is introducing himself to Roman believers and sharing his account of the gospel prior to visiting them for the first time.[46]

3. When is the event or conversation taking place?

   During Paul's third missionary journey, on his way to his final recorded trip to Jerusalem (Rom. 15:24-25), in the mid-to late AD 50s.[47]

4. Where is the event or conversation taking place?

   N/A

5. Why is the event or conversation taking place?

   Paul wrote this letter to formally introduce himself and explain the gospel to Christians who lived in Rome.[48]

6. How is the event or conversation taking place?

   Tertius, Paul's scribe, is writing Paul's letter to the Romans (Rom. 15:15; 16:22).

Step 3: INTERPRET

1. What does this text mean? What Timeless Life Lesson(s) do you believe God is trying to teach us?

_____

_____

---

[46] Andreas J. Kostenberger, L. Scott Kellum, and Charles L. Quarles, *The Cradle, The Cross, And Crown: An Introduction to the New Testament* (Nashville: B&H Academic, 2016), 600-601.

[47] Ibid., 594-595.

[48] Ibid., 597, 601.

2. Briefly describe your understanding of our source of joy and the benefits of choosing to be joyful.

Step 4: APPLY

1. What do you need to do? How will you specifically apply this lesson(s) to your life?

2. Journal additional thoughts God has placed on your heart regarding today's topic.

3. Write a prayer to God.

Day FIVE: Identifying Masks and Implementing Positive Changes

This is your final day of lesson 6. Can you recite this week's Courage Verse, Psalm 139:14, without looking at your card? At this mid-way point in our journey, are you finding it easier to memorize Scripture?

As we bring this week's lesson to a close, we want to look at the ways we often choose to hide our true selves and the positive changes we can make that will allow us to fully embrace who God created us to be.

Read the remainder of chapter 10 on pages 119 through 121 in *CFL*, "Unmask Your Authentic Identity," (beginning at the header "Exchange False Masks for True Identity").

Throughout Scripture, we read numerous accounts of godly men and women who covered up their true identities and experienced grave consequences as a result. In Genesis 12:9-20 and 20:1-18, Abraham convinces Sarah to disguise her identity (twice) because he feared for his life. In a similar way, we often cover up our true identity because we fear rejection or judgment.

Review the list, "The Masks We Wear," on pages 119 and 120 of chapter 10 in *CFL* and complete Action Step 1 of chapter 10, found on page 121 in *CFL*.

1. Action Step 1: Describe any masks you may be wearing and how they keep you from walking with a healthy identity.

   _____

   _____

   _____

   _____

   _____

   _____

   _____

2. Describe what you believe are the underlying reasons you wear masks.

   _____

   _____

   _____

   _____

   _____

   _____

Complete Action Step 2 of chapter 10, found on page 121 in *CFL*.

Action Step 2: Go to a quiet place where you can be alone with God and confess to Him the areas of your life you are covering up. Ask Him for wisdom and discernment regarding ways you might uncover them. Take at least five to ten minutes to be still and listen for God to speak to you.

3. Write down what you sense He is encouraging you to do and then make that your prayer for at least the next seven days. Don't rush this exercise.

_____

_____

_____

_____

_____

_____

_____

_____

_____

_____

_____

_____

_____

In addition to wearing masks, we often allow negative self-talk, which can contaminate everything we do. When we choose instead to think and speak positively about ourselves, we embrace God's view and gain additional courage to pursue His divine call on our lives.

While God cautions us not to think more highly of ourselves than we ought to think (Romans 12:3), He also reminds us to value our unique gifts and not allow them to go to waste. Read Romans 12:1-8, implement the Four Basic Bible Study Steps, and record your responses and findings. I have provided the Observation information to expedite your study process.

Step 1: PRAY

1. Begin by asking the Holy Spirit to guide you into all truth. Take a few minutes and write a prayer thanking God for His Word.

_____

_____

_____

_____

Step 2: OBSERVE

Romans 12:1-8

1. Who is speaking and being spoken to? Who is participating in the event?

   Paul, an Apostle and bond-servant of Christ (Rom. 1:1), is speaking to all who are beloved of God in Rome (Rom. 1:7).

2. What is happening? What is being said?

   Paul wrote to proclaim the gospel, to address problems within the Roman church, and to formally introduce himself before an upcoming visit.[49]

3. When is the event or conversation taking place?

   According to details in Acts and Romans, Paul likely wrote this letter near the end or after his third missionary journey, around AD 55 to 59.[50]

4. Where is the event or conversation taking place?

   N/A

5. Why is the event or conversation taking place?

   To urge believers to live life as in Christ, possessing unique gifts as a result of their salvation.

6. How is the event or conversation taking place?

   Paul is communicating with members of the Roman church by letter (Rom. 15:15).

7. Summarize how we are to view ourselves and utilize our individual gifts.

   _____

   _____

   _____

   _____

   _____

Step 3: INTERPRET

1. What does this text mean? What Timeless Life Lesson(s) do you believe God is trying to teach us?

   _____

   _____

   _____

   _____

---

[49] Anderas J. Kostenberger, L. Scott Kellum, and Charles L. Quarles, *The Cradle, The Cross, And Crown: An Introduction to the New Testament* (Nashville: B&H Academic, 2016), 601-603.

[50] Ibid., 594-595.

Step 4: APPLY

1. What do you need to do? How will you specifically apply this lesson(s) to your life?

_____

_____

_____

_____

Read the list of attributes below and list five to ten God-given gifts you possess, positive characteristics that allow you to impact your life and the lives of others in positive ways. God has gifted each one of us, and it's our responsibility to recognize and utilize our gifts. The following list is only meant to help you begin; there are many others.

- Encouragement
- Serving
- Hospitality
- Mercy
- Discernment
- Faith
- Teaching
- Creativity
- Leadership
- Entertaining
- Wisdom
- Compassion
- Faithfulness
- Dedication
- Perseverance

2. Once you have identified characteristics you possess, ask God to reveal other traits that make you unique. Remember, positive thinking is a choice. Therefore, think positively, rejoice over your valuable traits, and give thanks to God for allowing you to exercise them.

1. _____   6. _____

2. _____   7. _____

3. _____   8. _____

4. _____   9. _____

5. _____   10. _____

As each one has received a special gift,
employ it in serving one another as good stewards of the manifold grace of God.
—1 Peter 4:10

3. Describe your commitment to view yourself as God views you, employ positive self-thought and self-talk, and appreciate and utilize your God-given attributes and gifts.

_____

_____

_____

_____

_____

_____

_____

4. Journal additional thoughts God has placed on your heart regarding today's topic.

_____

_____

_____

_____

_____

_____

_____

5. Write a prayer to God.

_____

_____

_____

_____

_____

_____

_____

Congratulations! You've completed lesson 6 and have successfully made it half-way through our journey to courage together—and you've discovered the importance of adopting God's positive view of you. As Christians, we tend to misinterpret the concept of selflessness and putting others first. While we are called to be our brother's keeper and help those in need, we are never called to care for others at the expense of our own physical or emotional health. As you focused this week on the legitimacy of your God-given needs, you learned to identify your masks and manage your emotions. I pray you have courageously embraced who you truly are and have strengthened your God-given courage muscles in the process.

As we move on to lesson 7, "Replace Worldly Lies with Scriptural Truth," let's review and apply our Courage Quote, Courage Verse, and Timeless Life Lessons from this week's study.

LESSON 6

COURAGE QUOTE

REVIEW

To embrace life in true freedom, we must embrace ourselves with complete acceptance.

COURAGE VERSE

I will give thanks to You, for I am fearfully and wonderfully made;
Wonderful are Your works, and my soul knows it very well.

–Psalm 139:14

Timeless Life Lessons Learned

_____

_____

_____

_____

_____

_____

_____

_____

_____

_____

_____

R STEP IN COURAGE

LESSON 7

REPLACE WORLDLY LIES WITH SCRIPTURAL TRUTH

COURAGE QUOTE

Lies attack our character, our confidence, and our ability to make courageous changes.

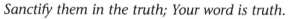

COURAGE VERSE

Sanctify them in the truth; Your word is truth.
As You sent Me into the world, I also have sent them into the world.
For their sakes I sanctify Myself, that they themselves also may be sanctified in truth.

–John 17:17-19

N ow that you have passed the half-way point in this study of the COURAGE steps, you are ready to tackle one of our most toxic opponents: the lies we believe. Over the past six weeks, we've worked diligently to begin making courageous changes in our lives. This week, we will focus on identifying the lies we believe about God, ourselves, our lives, our futures, and others. Once we identify and challenge these lies, we will learn to replace them with truth from God's Word—truth that ushers in change and fosters healing.

Our ability to defeat worldly lies relies heavily on our daily consumption of truth. Therefore, we will continue to strengthen our ability to discover and discern truth by studying Scripture and applying the Four Basic Bible Study Steps.

Day ONE: Uncovering Lies

Write this week's Courage Verse on a note card. Once again, place it where you will see it often and practice memorizing it throughout the week.

Read chapter 11 in *CFL*, "Replace Worldly Lies with Scriptural Truth." Complete Action Step 1 of chapter 11, found on page 132 in *CFL*.

1. Action Step 1: Open your Bible. Pray for God to convict you of any worldly lies you believe. Look up the following passages, write them on note cards, and read them daily until you have committed them to memory:

Colossians 2:8

2 Corinthians 10:5

Proverbs 3:5-6

In lesson 3, day 4, we studied Colossians 2:8 as we considered the importance of our Spiritual Health. Review your study of this passage and be prepared to complete step 3 of the Four Basic Bible Study Steps after you have observed the remaining two passages for today.

Read 2 Corinthians 10:5 and Proverbs 3:5-6 again, implement the Four Basic Bible Study Steps, and record your responses and findings. I have provided the Observation information to expedite your study process.

Step 1: PRAY

1. Begin by asking the Holy Spirit to guide you into all truth. Take a few minutes and write a prayer thanking God for His Word.

_____

_____

_____

Step 2: OBSERVE

2 Corinthians 10:5

1. Who is speaking and being spoken to? Who is participating in the event?

   Paul, an Apostle of Christ, is speaking to the church of Corinth and all the saints who are throughout Achaia (2 Cor. 1:1).

2. What is happening? What is being said?

   In 2 Corinthians, Paul is writing to believers to make them aware of changes in his travel plans (2 Cor. 1:15-17), to encourage the Corinthians to restore a church member to the congregation (2 Cor. 2:5-11), to encourage believers to contribute to the Jerusalem relief offering (2 Cor. 9:13), and to clear up any misunderstandings about his qualifications as an apostle of Christ (2 Cor. 11). In chapter 10, Paul is primarily describing himself to the Corinthians.

3. When is the event or conversation taking place?

   Paul is writing in AD 54-55 before his third visit to Corinth.[51]

4. Where is the event or conversation taking place?

   Paul is likely writing from Macedonia (2 Cor. 9:2).

5. Why is the event or conversation taking place?

   Because there were false apostles influencing believers in Corinth.[52]

---

[51] Andreas J. Kostenberger, L. Scott Kellum, and Charles L. Quarles, *The Cradle, The Cross, And Crown: An Introduction to the New Testament* (Nashville: B&H Academic, 2016), 546-547.

6. How is the event or conversation taking place?

Paul, with Timothy, is communicating with believers in Corinth by letter (2 Cor. 1:1,13; 9:1).

Proverbs 3:5-6

1. Who is speaking and being spoken to? Who is participating in the event?

In Proverbs 1-29, Solomon, the son of David, the King of Israel, is sharing wisdom with the Israelites (Prov. 1:1-2).[53]

2. What is happening? What is being said?

Solomon is sharing short statements, drawn from experience and full of wisdom and meaning, with the people of Israel.[54]

3. When is the event or conversation taking place?

Solomon is believed to have shared the wisdom sayings in Proverbs during his reign over Israel, during the first millennium BC.[55]

4. Where is the event or conversation taking place?

N/A

5. Why is the event or conversation taking place?

Solomon desires to instruct the people of Israel and to encourage them toward wise behavior (Prov. 1:1-6).

6. How is the event or conversation taking place?

N/A

Step 3: INTERPRET

1. What does these texts mean? What Timeless Life Lessons do you believe God is trying to teach us in these passages?

Colossians 2:8

---

[52] Ibid., 553-557.

[53] Eugene Merrill, Mark F. Rooker, & Michael A. Grisanti, *The World and the Word: An Introduction to the Old Testament* (Nashville: B&H Academic, 2011), 529.

[54] Frank E. Gaebelein, Willem VanGemern, Allen P. Ross, J. Stafford Wright, and Dennis F. Kinlaw, *The Expositor's Bible Commentary: Psalms, Proverbs, Ecclesiastes, Song of Songs.* Vol. 5. (Grand Rapids, MI: Zondervan Publishing House, 1991), 904.

[55] Eugene Merrill, Mark F. Rooker, and Michael A. Grisanti, *The World and the Word: An Introduction to the Old Testament* (Nashville: B&H Academic, 2011), 528.

2 Corinthians 10:5

Proverbs 3:5-6

Step 4: APPLY

1. What do you need to do? How will you specifically apply this lesson(s) to your life?

2. Journal additional thoughts God has placed on your heart regarding today's topic.

3. Write a prayer to God.

Day TWO: Putting Our Beliefs and Opinions in Perspective

Practice this week's Courage Verse, John 17:17-19.

When we neglect our growth in the knowledge and understanding of God's Word, we are unprotected and vulnerable to everyday temptations and lies. The more Scripture we know, the more prepared we are to make courageous, God-inspired choices.

Read Hosea 4:1-3, 6, implement the Four Basic Bible Study Steps, and record your responses and findings.

Step 1: PRAY

1. Begin by asking the Holy Spirit to guide you into all truth. Take a few minutes and write a prayer thanking God for His Word.

_____

_____

_____

_____

Step 2: OBSERVE

Hosea 4:1-3, 6

1. Who is speaking and being spoken to? Who is participating in the event?_____

_____

2. What is happening? What is being said? _____

_____

3. When is the event or conversation taking place? _____

_____

4. Where is the event or conversation taking place? _____

_____

5. Why is the event or conversation taking place?_____

_____

6. How is the event or conversation taking place?

_____

_____

Step 3: INTERPRET

1. What does this text mean? What Timeless Life Lesson(s) do you believe God is trying to teach us?

_____

_____

_____

_____

Step 4: APPLY

1. What do you need to do? How will you specifically apply this lesson(s) to your life?

_____

_____

_____

_____

Complete Action Step 2 of chapter 11, found on page 132 in _CFL_.

2. Action Step 2: Describe your commitment to discover truth from God's Word and replace any worldly lies you've adopted.

_____

_____

_____

_____

_____

_____

3. Journal additional thoughts God has placed on your heart regarding today's topic.

_____

_____

_____

_____

_____

_____

4. Write a prayer to God.

_____

_____

_____

_____

_____

_____

Day THREE: Discovering Truth

Practice this week's Courage Verse, John 17:17-19. Are you able to recite it without looking at your card? Try it and see.

To replace worldly lies with scriptural truth, we must not only be able to recognize the lie, but we must also be able to discern the truth in God's Word.

Just as we discussed in lesson 1, we will encounter misunderstandings and misinterpretations of Scripture throughout our lives, either by misreading it ourselves or adopting the beliefs and opinions of others who (intentionally or unintentionally) misquote Scripture. Over the past six weeks, we've worked diligently to learn effective study habits that will help us avoid misunderstandings as often as possible. Now that you've consistently practiced the Four Basic Bible Study Steps for the past six weeks, you are better prepared to tackle frequently misinterpreted passages.

Today and tomorrow, I want you to study two familiar passages that are often misunderstood: Jeremiah 29:11 and Romans 8:28. For today, write Jeremiah 29:11 and describe your initial understanding of this verse.

_____

_____

_____

Implement the Four Basic Bible Study Steps and record your responses and findings.

Step 1: PRAY

1. Begin by asking the Holy Spirit to guide you into all truth. Take a few minutes and write a prayer thanking God for His Word.

_____

_____

_____

_____

Step 2: OBSERVE

Jeremiah 29:11

1. Who is speaking and being spoken to? Who is participating in the event? _____

    _____

2. What is happening? What is being said? _____

    _____

3. When is the event or conversation taking place? _____

    _____

4. Where is the event or conversation taking place? _____

    _____

5. Why is the event or conversation taking place? _____

    _____

6. How is the event or conversation taking place?

    _____

    _____

    _____

Step 3: INTERPRET

1. What does this text mean? What Timeless Life Lesson(s) do you believe God is trying to teach us?

    _____

    _____

    _____

    _____

    _____

Step 4: APPLY

1. What do you need to do? How will you specifically apply this lesson(s) to your life?

    _____

    _____

    _____

    _____

2. Do your findings support your initial understanding of this verse? Did you discover a lie or distorted belief that you need to replace? Explain.

_____

_____

_____

_____

3. Journal additional thoughts God has placed on your heart regarding today's topic.

_____

_____

_____

_____

_____

_____

4. Write a prayer to God.

_____

_____

_____

_____

_____

Day FOUR: Sharpening Our Skills

Practice this week's Courage Verse, John 17:17-19. Now try to recite it entirely from memory without glancing at your card. How did you do?

Since proper Bible study and accurate interpretation skills are paramount to our ability to distinguish worldly lies from scriptural truth, let's continue practicing. Yesterday we studied a well-known passage that is often misunderstood, Jeremiah 29:11. Today we will study a second well-known passage that is often misunderstood, Romans 8:28. Write Romans 8:28 and describe your initial understanding of this verse.

_____

_____

_____

Implement the Four Basic Bible Study Steps and record your responses and findings.

Step 1: PRAY

1. Begin by asking the Holy Spirit to guide you into all truth. Take a few minutes and write a prayer thanking God for His Word.

_____

_____

_____

_____

_____

Step 2: OBSERVE

Romans 8:28

1. Who is speaking and being spoken to? Who is participating in the event? _____

_____

2. What is happening? What is being said? _____

_____

3. When is the event or conversation taking place? _____

_____

4. Where is the event or conversation taking place? _____

_____

5. Why is the event or conversation taking place? _____

_____

6. How is the event or conversation taking place?

_____

_____

Step 3: INTERPRET

1. What does this text mean? What Timeless Life Lesson(s) do you believe God is trying to teach us?

_____

_____

_____

_____

Step 4: APPLY

1. What do you need to do? How will you specifically apply this lesson(s) to your life?

_____

_____

_____

_____

2. Do your findings support your initial understanding of this verse? Did you discover a lie or distorted belief that you need to replace? Explain.

_____

_____

_____

_____

3. Journal additional thoughts God has placed on your heart regarding today's topic.

_____

_____

_____

_____

_____

_____

_____

4. Write a prayer to God.

_____

_____

_____

_____

_____

_____

_____

Day FIVE: Replacing Lies with Truth

This is your final day of lesson 7. Can you recite this week's Courage Verse, John 17:17-19, without looking at your card? If so, give yourself another high five!

Throughout these past seven weeks, you've likely uncovered some of the lies you are tempted to believe and have learned how to more accurately discover truth in the Bible. Today, I want to lead you through a practical exercise that will assist you in replacing worldly lies and retaining God's truth in your mind and heart instead.

As I mention on page 131 of chapter 11 in *CFL*, when we receive new information that challenges our beliefs, we have the option of employing five various responses:

1. Accept it (believe it).

2. Ignore it (deny it).

3. Question it (challenge it).

4. Blend it (merge it into our current belief).

5. Replace it (change what we believe entirely).

Once we have clearly determined the truth, we see only two responses that, put together, allow us to grow and mature into the godly women and men God calls us to be. That is, we must *accept the truth* and *replace the lie*.

Remember, it takes courage to admit we've been wrong and replace our worldly beliefs with scriptural truth. Even so, we must exercise our courage muscles and choose to accept God's Word.

Read Chapter 12 in *CFL*, "Recognize the Truth Trifecta." Complete Action Step 1 of chapter 12, found on page 139 in *CFL*.

1. Action Step 1: In the first column, make a list of the lies you've identified over the last seven weeks. Then, in the second column, write a biblical verse that replaces the lie with truth. If you are unsure what verse appropriately replaces your lie, refer to the list on pages 137 through 139 of *CFL* for suggestions. You can also ask a friend, loved one, or spiritual mentor for help.

Remember: Don't attempt to make Scripture fit your belief. Instead, conform your belief to fit the truth found in Scripture.

Worldly Lies	Scriptural Truth

Now that you have charted your lies and truth, it's time to insert them into an exercise recommended by my life coach and dear friend, Robbie Goss. This is an exercise I used—and still use to this day—to exchange damaging lies for truth.

On the following Lies and Truth Exercise cards, insert each lie you've believed into the first blank. On the second blank, summarize the scriptural truth you've discovered and then, under the header "Scripture Reference," write out the verse that overcomes your lie.

Read your lies and truths at least once a day. Meditate on the truths and denounce the lies in the name of Jesus. Do this exercise for at least thirty days, but preferably for sixty days. I've included several blank cards for you to use. Of course, you can also make your own on note cards.

Lie & Truth Exercise:

I reject the Lie that:

_____
_____
_____

The Truth is:

_____
_____
_____

Scripture Reference:

_____
_____
_____

Lie & Truth Exercise:

I reject the Lie that:

_____
_____
_____

The Truth is:

_____
_____
_____

Scripture Reference:

_____
_____
_____

Lie & Truth Exercise:

I reject the Lie that:

_____
_____
_____

The Truth is:

_____
_____
_____

Scripture Reference:

_____
_____
_____

Lie & Truth Exercise:

I reject the Lie that:

_____
_____
_____

The Truth is:

_____
_____
_____

Scripture Reference:

_____
_____
_____

Lie & Truth Exercise:

I reject the Lie that:

_____
_____
_____

The Truth is:

_____
_____
_____

Scripture Reference:

_____
_____
_____

Lie & Truth Exercise:

I reject the Lie that:

_____
_____
_____

The Truth is:

_____
_____
_____

Scripture Reference:

_____
_____
_____

We discussed the importance of nurturing our Spiritual Health in lesson 3. To grow spiritually, we must set aside at least fifteen minutes each day to spend quiet time with God. We must also be in His Word daily and challenge ourselves through regular study of the Bible.

I neglected to grow in my knowledge and understanding of God and His Word for about twenty years after praying to receive Christ. I had no clue what to do or how to go about growing spiritually. Frankly, I didn't even understand why I needed to. Years later, several friends encouraged me to grow closer to God, and because of their loving encouragement, I read and studied the Bible more often and grew much closer to God. My friends continued to encourage and disciple me through the years, and as I became more spiritually mature, I felt led by God to encourage and disciple others.

It's always a good practice to engage in a discipleship relationship with someone who is further along in his/her spiritual journey—and we should always be looking for opportunities to encourage and disciple others in the same way.

Complete Action Step 2 of chapter 12, found on page 139 in *CFL*. Seek out a spiritually mature Christian and ask to meet with him/her weekly for discipleship while you complete the Lies and Truth Exercise. A wise mentor can strengthen your understanding of biblical truth. If possible, maintain this relationship after the recommended time of thirty to sixty days.

2. Write the name of your spiritual mentor on the following lines, along with your commitment to disciple with him/her on a regular basis.

_____

_____

_____

_____

3. Journal additional thoughts God has placed on your heart regarding today's topic.

_____

_____

_____

_____

_____

_____

_____

4. Write a prayer to God.

_____

_____

_____

_____

_____

_____

_____

Congratulations! You've completed lesson 7, worked diligently to sharpen your inductive study skills, and started the important process of replacing harmful lies with life-giving truth.

As we move on to lesson 8, "Accept the Things You Cannot Change," let's review and apply our Courage Quote, Courage Verse, and Timeless Life Lessons from this week's study and allow God's Word to give us a new sense of hope, inspiration, and courage for life.

LESSON 7

REVIEW

COURAGE QUOTE

Lies attack our character, our confidence, and our ability to make courageous changes.

COURAGE VERSE

Sanctify them in the truth; Your word is truth.
As You sent Me into the world, I also have sent them into the world.
For their sakes I sanctify Myself, that they themselves also may be sanctified in truth.

–John 17:17-19

Timeless Life Lessons Learned

_____

_____

_____

_____

_____

_____

_____

_____

_____

_____

_____

A STEP IN COURAGE

ACCEPT THE THINGS YOU CANNOT CHANGE

Acceptance is often as difficult as change, requiring just as much courage and sometimes demanding a lot more determination.

Do not store up for yourselves treasures on earth, where moth and rust destroy, and where thieves break in and steal. But store up for yourselves treasures in heaven, where neither moth nor rust destroys, and where thieves do not break in or steal; for where your treasure is, there your heart will be also.

–Matthew 6:19-21

We have come a long way over the past seven weeks and have worked through several difficult steps, making necessary commitments, overcoming obstacles, embracing our true identity, and reconciling lies and misunderstandings. This week, we will tackle another difficult component of exercising courage: acceptance.

Change is always hard and requires a spirit of fearlessness, but accepting things that may never change can force our courage muscles to work overtime. The key to success in this important step is making an honest assessment of each situation and then courageously choosing the proper response.

Day ONE: Considering Circumstances

Write this week's Courage Verse on a note card. Place it where you will see it often and practice memorizing it throughout the week.

Read chapter 13 in *CFL*, "Accept the Things You Cannot Change." Complete Action Step 1 of chapter 13, found on page 154 in *CFL* and add this to your daily routine this week.

1. Action Step 1: Take out two note cards and write the most common version of the Serenity Prayer, quoted on page 144 of *CFL*, on each card. Place the cards in the same area (or areas) you place your Scripture Memorization note cards. Recite this prayer daily for at least seven days and strive to memorize it.

On pages 144 and 145 of *CFL* review the "Changeable vs. Unchangeable Life Experiences" list. Complete Action Step 2 of chapter 13, found on page 154 in *CFL*.

2. Action Step 2: Create your own changeable vs. unchangeable chart. Spend time in prayer and communication with God. Ask Him to give you the wisdom to discern the things you can and cannot change. Then, in the chart below, list the things in your life you can and cannot change.

Changeable	Unchangeable

3. Journal additional thoughts God has placed on your heart regarding today's topic.

_____

_____

_____

_____

_____

_____

4. Write a prayer to God.

_____

_____

_____

_____

_____

_____

_____

_____

Day TWO: Preparing for Acceptance and/or Action

Practice this week's Courage Verse, Matthew 6:19-21, and the Serenity Prayer.

Once we discern the difference between the changeable and unchangeable aspects of our life, we can then courageously implement one of two primary responses: acceptance and/or action.

Read the account of Abigail and Nabal in 1 Samuel 25:2-38, implement the Four Basic Bible Study Steps, and record your responses and findings.

Step 1: PRAY

1. Begin by asking the Holy Spirit to guide you into all truth. Take a few minutes and write a prayer thanking God for His Word.

_____

_____

_____

_____

Step 2: OBSERVE

1 Samuel 25:2-38

1. Who is speaking and being spoken to? Who is participating in the event? _____

   _____

2. What is happening? What is being said? _____

   _____

3. When is the event or conversation taking place? _____

   _____

4. Where is the event or conversation taking place? _____

   _____

5. Why is the event or conversation taking place? _____

   _____

6. How is the event or conversation taking place?

   _____

   _____

7. Describe Abigail's predicament and her response to her situation.

   _____

   _____

   _____

   _____

   _____

   _____

8. Did Abigail respond with acceptance, action, or both? Explain.

   _____

   _____

   _____

   _____

   _____

   _____

Step 3: INTERPRET

1. What does this text mean? What Timeless Life Lesson(s) do you believe God is trying to teach us?

Step 4: APPLY

1. What do you need to do? How will you specifically apply this lesson(s) to your life?

2. Journal additional thoughts God has placed on your heart regarding today's topic.

3. Write a prayer to God.

Day THREE: Accepting Responsibility

Practice this week's Courage Verse, Matthew 6:19-21, and the Serenity Prayer. Are you able to recite either of them without looking at your cards? Try it and see.

While we can't control how others act, react, or respond, we can courageously choose our own actions, reactions, and responses. While it's not our job to manage the perspectives and pursuits of others, it is our responsibility to carefully consider the prudence of our own choices and monitor our own contentedness. We can choose where to place our focus.

1. Read and write the following passages.

   Galatians 6:5-9

   _____

   _____

   _____

   Philippians 4:11-12

   _____

   _____

   _____

   2 Corinthians 4:16-18

   _____

   _____

   _____

Read Galatians 6:5-9, Philippians 4:11-12, and 2 Corinthians 4:16-18 again, implement the Four Basic Bible Study Steps, and record your responses and findings. I have provided the Observation information to expedite your study process.

Step 1: PRAY

1. Begin by asking the Holy Spirit to guide you into all truth. Take a few minutes and write a prayer thanking God for His Word.

   _____

   _____

   _____

   _____

Step 2: OBSERVE

Galatians 6:5-9

1. Who is speaking and being spoken to? Who is participating in the event?

   Paul, an Apostle of Christ, is speaking to the churches of Galatia (Gal. 1:1-2).

2. What is happening? What is being said?

   Paul teaches against salvation based on man's ability and efforts to keep God's law.[56]

3. When is the event or conversation taking place?

   Galatians was most likely written in AD 48-49.[57]

4. Where is the event or conversation taking place?

   N/A

5. Why is the event or conversation taking place?

   Soon after Paul left Galatia, false teachers made their way into the churches and began distorting the gospel by insisting believers must also keep the law of Moses.[58]

6. How is the event or conversation taking place?

   Paul is communicating with the Galatians by letter (Gal. 1:20).

Philippians 4:11-12

1. Who is speaking and being spoken to? Who is participating in the event?

   Paul, a bond-servant of Christ, is speaking to believers, including overseers and deacons, in Philippi (Phil. 1:1).

2. What is happening? What is being said?

   Paul urges believers to live in harmony, having the same attitude as Christ (Phil. 2:1-5). He warns them to disregard lessons taught by false teachers (Phil. 3:2), and he addresses issues caused by two women in the church, Euodia and Syntyche (Phil. 4:2-3).

3. When is the event or conversation taking place?

   Likely sometime between AD 50 to AD 63.[59]

4. Where is the event or conversation taking place?

   Philippians is considered a Prison Epistle; most scholars believe Paul likely wrote this letter during his imprisonment in Rome (Phil. 1:12-13).[60]

5. Why is the event or conversation taking place?

   Paul wanted to encourage believers to partner with one another in the gospel and live a life worthy of Christ's sacrifice.[61]

---

[56] Andreas J. Kostenberger, L. Scott Kellum, and Charles L. Quarles, *The Cradle, The Cross, And Crown: An Introduction to the New Testament* (Nashville: B&H Academic, 2016), 483.

[57] Ibid., 494.

[58] Ibid. 495.

[59] Andreas J. Kostenberger, L. Scott Kellum, and Charles L. Quarles, *The Cradle, The Cross, And Crown: An Introduction to the New Testament* (Nashville: B&H Academic, 2016), 641.

[60] Ibid., 644-645.

6. How is the event or conversation taking place?

   Paul is communicating with believers in Philippi by letter (Phil. 3:3).

2 Corinthians 4:16-18

1. Who is speaking and being spoken to? Who is participating in the event?

   Paul, an Apostle of Christ, is speaking to the church of Corinth and all the saints who are throughout Achaia (2 Cor. 1:1).

2. What is happening? What is being said?

   In 2 Corinthians, Paul is writing to believers to make them aware of changes in his travel plans (2 Cor. 1:15-17), to encourage the Corinthians to restore a church member to the congregation (2 Cor. 2:5-11), to encourage believers to contribute to the Jerusalem relief offering (2 Cor. 9:13), and to clear up any misunderstandings about his qualifications as an apostle of Christ (2 Cor. 11). In chapter 10, Paul is primarily describing himself to the Corinthians.

3. When is the event or conversation taking place?

   Paul is writing in AD 54-55 before his third visit to Corinth.[62]

4. Where is the event or conversation taking place?

   Paul is likely writing from Macedonia (2 Cor. 9:2).

5. Why is the event or conversation taking place?

   Because there were false apostles influencing believers in Corinth.[63]

6. How is the event or conversation taking place?

   Paul, with Timothy, is communicating with believers in Corinth by means of a letter (2 Cor. 1:1,13; 9:1).

7. In what ways do these verses encourage you to embrace acceptance or take action?

   _____

   _____

   _____

   _____

   _____

   _____

   _____

   _____

   _____

---

[61] Ibid., 646.

[62] Andreas J. Kostenberger, L. Scott Kellum, and Charles L. Quarles, *The Cradle, The Cross, And Crown: An Introduction to the New Testament* (Nashville: B&H Academic, 2016), 546-547.

[63] Ibid., 553-557.

Step 3: INTERPRET

1. What does these texts mean? What Timeless Life Lessons do you believe God is trying to teach us?

    Galatians 6:5-9

    _____

    _____

    _____

    Philippians 4:11-12

    _____

    _____

    _____

    2 Corinthians 4:16-18

    _____

    _____

    _____

    _____

Step 4: APPLY

1. What do you need to do? How will you specifically apply these lessons to your life?

    _____

    _____

    _____

2. Journal additional thoughts God has placed on your heart regarding today's topic.

    _____

    _____

    _____

    _____

3. Write a prayer to God.

_____

_____

_____

_____

_____

Day FOUR: Maintaining a Courageous Perspective

Practice this week's Courage Verse, Matthew 6:19-21, and the Serenity Prayer. Now try to recite both entirely from memory without glancing at your cards. How did you do?

No matter what challenge or circumstance we face, we have the option—the choice—to focus either on the problems or the possibilities.

Today, we will consider the composure and choices of Daniel, a very courageous individual who faced both promising and dire circumstances with great courage and confidence. Read chapters 1 and 6 in the book of Daniel, implement the Four Basic Bible Study Steps, and record your responses and findings.

Step 1: PRAY

1. Begin by asking the Holy Spirit to guide you into all truth. Take a few minutes and write a prayer thanking God for His Word.

_____

_____

_____

Step 2: OBSERVE

Daniel 1

1. Who is speaking and being spoken to? Who is participating in the event?_____

_____

2. What is happening? What is being said? _____

_____

3. When is the event or conversation taking place? _____

_____

4. Where is the event or conversation taking place? _____

_____

5. Why is the event or conversation taking place? _____

_____

6. How is the event or conversation taking place?

_____

_____

Daniel 6

1. Who is speaking and being spoken to? Who is participating in the event? _____

_____

2. What is happening? What is being said? _____

_____

3. When is the event or conversation taking place? _____

_____

4. Where is the event or conversation taking place? _____

_____

5. Why is the event or conversation taking place? _____

_____

6. How is the event or conversation taking place?

_____

_____

7. Describe how Daniel responded to his circumstances. Explain how he embraced his situation and carefully considered his choices.

_____

_____

Step 3: INTERPRET

1. What do these passages from Daniel mean? What Timeless Life Lessons do you believe God is trying to teach us?

_____

_____

_____

_____

Step 4: APPLY

1. What do you need to do? How will you specifically apply this lesson(s) to your life?

_____

_____

_____

_____

As we have seen, most circumstances require both acceptance and action. So, before we close out today's lesson, take a few minutes and review your chart of changeable vs. unchangeable from day 1. Then, in the chart below, describe what you will strive to accept and ways you will take action.

What I Will Strive to Accept	How I Will Take Action

2. Journal additional thoughts God has placed on your heart regarding today's topic.

_____

_____

_____

_____

_____

_____

_____

3. Write a prayer to God.

_____

_____

_____

_____

_____

_____

_____

_____

Day FIVE: Breaking Free from the Presence of Pain

This is your final day of lesson 7. Can you recite this week's Courage Verse, Matthew 6:19-21, and the Serenity Prayer without looking at your cards? If so, give yourself a high five!

This week, we've exercised our courage muscles in the areas of acceptance and action. We've analyzed our circumstances and relationships to determine the proper response, and we've challenged ourselves to implement biblical principles that will help us embrace the reality and possibilities of the choices available to us.

We've discussed the importance of accepting the reality of sin, suffering, and the seasons of life, and we've talked about the essential steps to overcoming pain. We will conclude this week's lesson by working through the Nine Steps to Dealing with Pain, recommended by LifeBuilders counselor Robbie Goss.

As I mention on page 146 of *CFL*, we can break free from the bondage of past trauma and sin when we make the choice to implement these steps, develop our personal relationship with Christ, and connect with counselors and others who will support us in the process.

Review the "Nine Steps to Dealing with Pain" on pages 146 and 147 of *CFL*, work through each step and journal your answers to the following questions.

Step 1: Allow yourself to feel the full weight of the pain.

Spend the next five to ten minutes in prayer and reflection. Ask God to help you identify painful areas of your life and/or past that you've never properly worked through.

1. Describe these areas of your life/past and exercise the first step in dealing with pain: allow yourself to feel the full weight of the pain.

_____

_____

_____

_____

_____

_____

_____

Step 2: Express your primary emotions to God and trusted, safe friends.

In chapter 10 of *CFL*, we discussed the difference between surface feelings (secondary emotions) and underlying feelings (primary emotions). Review the list "Surface Feelings vs. Underlying Feelings" on page 118 of chapter 10 in *CFL* and identify the primary emotions you experience as a result of your pain. Spend several minutes in prayer, expressing your primary emotions to God.

1. Describe your primary emotions and write the name of your safe friend or loved one with whom you will share your pain and emotions.

_____

_____

_____

_____

_____

_____

Step 3: Recognize the original source of your pain.

Spend a few more minutes in prayer and reflection. Ask God to help you identify the source of your past or present pain.

1. Describe the source of your pain.

_____

_____

_____

_____

_____

_____

_____

Step 4: Receive healing from the Lord for your specific damaged feelings.

Once again, spend some time in prayer with God. Claim His promises from specific passages of Scripture, stated below, and embrace His comforting and healing presence.

God's promise from Isaiah 41:10:

Do not fear your circumstances or other people, God is with you always. You can face your trials with courage because God will strengthen and help you through them.

God's promise from Psalm 103:1-5:

God will pardon your sin, heal your spiritual and physical conditions according to His will, redeem your life through His lovingkindness and compassion, and will give you strength for life throughout your years.

God's promise from Psalm 147:3:

God will heal your broken heart and bind up your wounds when you repent and turn/return to Him.

1. Describe how you plan to embrace these promises.

_____

_____

_____

_____

_____

_____

Step 5: Release your pain back to the cross.

Spend time in prayer with God. Recognize that Christ's suffering and sacrifice set us free to stand firm. We can reject enslavement to our pain (Gal. 5:1; Rom. 8:15).

1. Write your commitment to leave your pain at the foot of the cross and walk in God-given freedom.

_____

_____

_____

_____

_____

_____

Step 6: Rescue the part of you that you rejected at the point of your pain.

Spend the next three to five minutes in prayer with God. Ask Him to help you identify areas of your identity you've rejected.

1. Describe your personal rejection and your commitment to redeem your worth.

_____

_____

_____

_____

_____

Steps 7 and 8: Reject the lies that came from your pain and replace the lies with specific truth from God's Word.

In lesson 6, we practiced replacing our worldly lies with scriptural truth. Spend several minutes reviewing the lies and truths you discovered last week.

1. Identify the lies specifically associated with your pain. Write the lies and scriptural truths below and then practice replacing your lies with the truth.

_____

_____

_____

_____

_____

Step 9: Release your offender by forgiving him/her.

Forgiveness is a major component of our pursuit of freedom from our pain. It is one of the most courageous choices we can make and allows us to release our offenders and move forward with our lives.

Forgiveness doesn't mean we compromise healthy boundaries. Rather, forgiveness means we accept the reality that we live in a sinful, fallen world and are sinful, fallen people. In light of this understanding, we must courageously choose to let go of any anger and pain associated with the offense. We are called to release our offenders from their debt.

Spend time asking God to forgive your unforgiveness and to help you strive to forgive those who have hurt you.

1. List the names of those you need to forgive. Pray for each one daily for at least the next seven days.

2. Journal additional thoughts God has placed on your heart regarding today's topic.

3. Write a prayer to God.

Congratulations! You've completed lesson 8 and courageously worked to recognize the difference between acceptance and action. You've considered biblical accounts that encourage you to maintain a courageous perspective, and you've worked through nine steps to begin dealing with lingering pain in your life.

As we move on to lesson 9, "Grasp God's Love for You," let's review and apply our Courage Quote, Courage Verse, and Timeless Life Lessons from this week's study. It's time to embrace our newfound ability to accept the things we cannot change and change the things we can.

REVIEW

Acceptance is often as difficult as change, requiring just as much courage and sometimes demanding a lot more determination.

Do not store up for yourselves treasures on earth, where moth and rust destroy, and where thieves break in and steal. But store up for yourselves treasures in heaven, where neither moth nor rust destroys, and where thieves do not break in or steal; for where your treasure is, there your heart will be also.
–Matthew 6:19-21

Timeless Life Lessons Learned

_____

_____

_____

_____

_____

_____

_____

_____

_____

G STEP IN COURAGE

GRASP GOD'S LOVE FOR YOU

We all desire a love that is unconditional, available, consistent, and everlasting. God's love is all of the above and so much more—if we choose to embrace it.

For I am convinced that neither death, nor life, nor angels, nor principalities, nor things present, nor things to come, nor powers, nor height, nor depth, nor any other created thing, will be able to separate us from the love of God, which is in Christ Jesus our Lord.

–Romans 8:38-39

By now, you are a pro at implementing the inductive Bible study process, and you've most surely strengthened your courage muscles over the past eight weeks. As we near completion of our courage journey together, it is important we completely understand and accept God's abundant love and grace.

During this week's lesson, we will focus on fully embracing the magnitude of God's love. In the process, we will evaluate our devotion to God and our understanding of His unwavering desire to draw us ever closer into personal relationship with Him. Unless we fully grasp the assurance and depth of God's love for us, we will remain vulnerable to doubt, distractions, discouragement, and detours.

Day ONE: Seeing God

Write this week's Courage Verse, Romans 8:38-39, on a note card. Place it where you will see it often and practice memorizing it throughout the week.

Read chapter 14 in *CFL*, "Grasp God's Love for You." Complete the first question in Action Step 1 of chapter 14, found on page 168 in *CFL*.

1. Action Step 1a: Take an honest assessment of how you see God. Describe your view.

_____

_____

_____

_____

_____

Read Jeremiah 9:23-24, implement the Four Basic Bible Study Steps, and record your responses and findings.

Step 1: PRAY

1. Begin by asking the Holy Spirit to guide you into all truth. Take a few minutes and write a prayer thanking God for His Word.

_____

_____

_____

_____

Step 2: OBSERVE

Jeremiah 9:23-24

1. Who is speaking and being spoken to? Who is participating in the event?_____

_____

2. What is happening? What is being said? _____

_____

3. When is the event or conversation taking place? _____

_____

4. Where is the event or conversation taking place? _____

_____

5. Why is the event or conversation taking place?_____

_____

6. How is the event or conversation taking place?

_____

_____

7. Describe what you learn about God and our responsibility to genuinely know Him.

_____

_____

_____

_____

Step 3: INTERPRET

1. What does this text mean? What Timeless Life Lesson(s) do you believe God is trying to teach us?

_____

_____

_____

_____

Step 4: APPLY

1. What do you need to do? How will you specifically apply this lesson(s) to your life?

_____

_____

_____

_____

2. Journal additional thoughts God has placed on your heart regarding today's topic.

_____

_____

_____

_____

_____

_____

3. Write a prayer to God.

_____

_____

_____

_____

_____

_____

Day TWO: Believing in God

Practice this week's Courage Verse, Romans 8:38-39.

On page 158 of chapter 14 in *CFL*, I describe the four stages of how we see God, the importance of investing in our spiritual growth journey, and the value of actively nurturing our personal relationship with Him.

Yesterday, we reviewed the first stage of how we see God, through our *view of* Him. Today, we will discuss stage 2 of how we see God, through our *belief in* Him.

Some people completely dismiss the reality of God. Others believe He exists, but don't see Him as personally relatable. Let's take an honest look at what Scripture says and compare it to what we genuinely believe.

Read Hebrews 11:1, 6, implement the Four Basic Bible Study Steps, and record your responses and findings.

Step 1: PRAY

1. Begin by asking the Holy Spirit to guide you into all truth. Take a few minutes and write a prayer thanking God for His Word.

_____

_____

_____

_____

_____

Step 2: OBSERVE

Hebrews 11:1, 6

1. Who is speaking and being spoken to? Who is participating in the event? _____

_____

2. What is happening? What is being said? _____

_____

3. When is the event or conversation taking place? _____

_____

4. Where is the event or conversation taking place? _____

_____

5. Why is the event or conversation taking place? _____

_____

6. How is the event or conversation taking place?

_____

_____

7. What do you learn about faith in this passage?

_____

_____

_____

_____

Step 3: INTERPRET

1. What does this text mean? What Timeless Life Lesson(s) do you believe God is trying to teach us?

_____

_____

_____

_____

_____

Step 4: APPLY

1. What do you need to do? How will you specifically apply this lesson(s) to your life?

_____

_____

_____

_____

_____

Do you remember the first time you surrendered your life to God, the day you fully embraced the reality of His existence, repented of your sin, and asked Christ to be Lord and Savior of your life?

If you've never fully accepted God's existence and surrendered your life to Him, there's no better time than now to do so. In chapter 13 of *CFL*, I included the section "Accepting Salvation" on pages 152 through 154. If you are not sure you've received Christ as your personal Lord and Savior, I invite you to pray the short prayer printed on page 153 in *CFL* and ask God to enter your heart and transform your life.

2. Describe your salvation experience, whether in the past or in this very moment.

    _____

    _____

    _____

    _____

    _____

3. Is your love for God as passionate as when you believed and received Him for the very first time? Or has it weakened through the years as a result of the trials and busyness of everyday life? Explain.

    _____

    _____

    _____

    _____

    _____

    _____

4. Journal additional thoughts God has placed on your heart regarding today's topic.

    _____

    _____

    _____

    _____

    _____

5. Write a prayer to God.

    _____

    _____

    _____

    _____

    _____

Day THREE: Accepting God

Practice this week's Courage Verse, Romans 8:38-39. Are you able to recite it without looking at your card? Try it and see.

Today we will discuss stage 3 of how we see God, which is through our *acceptance of* Him.

Hebrews 13:8 tells us that "Jesus Christ is the same yesterday and today and forever." The attributes of God expressed in the Old Testament and New Testament are the same attributes of God today.

1. Read and write the following passages:

2 Peter 3:9

_____

_____

_____

Isaiah 40:28-29

_____

_____

_____

John 14:6

_____

_____

_____

Read each passage again, implement the Four Basic Bible Study Steps, and record your responses and findings. I have provided the Observation information to expedite your study process.

Step 1: PRAY

1. Begin by asking the Holy Spirit to guide you into all truth. Take a few minutes and write a prayer thanking God for His Word.

_____

_____

_____

_____

_____

Step 2: OBSERVE

2 Peter 3:9

1. Who is speaking and being spoken to? Who is participating in the event?

   Simon Peter, an apostle of Christ, is speaking to Gentile believers in northern Asia Minor (modern day Turkey).[64]

2. What is happening? What is being said?

   Simon Peter is addressing false teaching in the churches (2 Pet. 2:1).

3. When is the event or conversation taking place?

   Most likely right before Peter was martyred.[65]

4. Where is the event or conversation taking place?

   N/A

5. Why is the event or conversation taking place?

   To warn believers to be aware of false teachers and protect themselves from falling prey to dishonest teaching (2 Pet. 3:17).

6. How is the event or conversation taking place?

   Simon Peter is communicating with believers by letter (2 Pet. 3:1).

Isaiah 40:28-29

1. Who is speaking and being spoken to? Who is participating in the event?

   God, through the Prophet Isaiah, is speaking to the people of Israel (Is. 40:1, 27).

2. What is happening? What is being said?

   God is stating the questions He knows the Israelites are asking, and He is providing them with answers.[66]

3. When is the event or conversation taking place?

   Isaiah prophesied during the reigns of four Judean kings who ruled Israel from about 739-700 BC. This period was prior to Babylon conquering Judah in 605 BC (Is. 39:6-7) and during a time when Israel made and worshiped idols (Is. 44:9-20, 46:6-7, 48:5, 57:5, 66:3, 17).[67]

4. Where is the event or conversation taking place?

   In Judah and Jerusalem (Is. 1:1).

5. Why is the event or conversation taking place?

   To encourage the Israelites to reflect on God's answers to their questions and to give them courage and instructions to endure their coming judgment and captivity.[68]

---

[64] Andreas J. Kostenberger, L. Scott Kellum, and Charles L. Quarles, *The Cradle, The Cross, And Crown: An Introduction to the New Testament* (Nashville: B&H Academic, 2016), 840, 864.

[65] Ibid., 863.

[66] Gary Smith, The New American Commentary: *Isaiah 40-66*, Vol. 15B (Nashville: Broadman & Holman Publishers, 2009), 106.

[67] Eugene Merrill, Mark F. Rooker, and Michael A. Grisanti, *The World and the Word: An Introduction to the Old Testament* (Nashville: B&H Academic, 2011), 367.

[68] Gary Smith, *The New American Commentary: Isaiah 40-66*, Vol. 15B (Nashville: Broadman & Holman Publishers, 2009), 106.

6. How is the event or conversation taking place?

    Isaiah communicated and wrote down messages God gave him regarding present and future plans for the Israelites, foreign nations, and all the world.[69]

John 14:6

1. Who is speaking and being spoken to? Who is participating in the event?

    Jesus is speaking to His disciples (Jn. 11:16, 14:5-6, 20:24).

2. What is happening? What is being said?

    Jesus is answering a question that Thomas, one of His disciples, had asked (Jn. 14:5).

3. When is the event or conversation taking place?

    In chapter 14, Jesus is speaking to His disciples shortly before He is arrested (Jn. 18:12), accused, beaten (19:1-3), and crucified (19:17-18).

4. Where is the event or conversation taking place?

    Jerusalem (Jn. 12:12).

5. Why is the event or conversation taking place?

    Jesus is comforting His disciples and preparing them for His departure and crucifixion (Jn. 14:1-3).

6. How is the event or conversation taking place?

    Jesus is speaking directly to His disciples, right after sharing His last supper with them (Jn. 13:1-2).

7. What attributes of God do you discover in these three passages?

    _____

    _____

    _____

Step 3: INTERPRET

1. What do these texts mean? What Timeless Life Lessons do you believe God is trying to teach us?

    2 Peter 3:9

    _____

    _____

    _____

    Isaiah 40:28-29

    _____

    _____

    _____

---

69 Ibid., 41.

John 14:6

_____

_____

_____

Step 4: APPLY

1. What do you need to do? How will you specifically apply these lessons to your life?

_____

_____

_____

_____

2. Do you fully accept God's unchanging attributes? How do His attributes impact your everyday life?

_____

_____

_____

_____

3. Journal additional thoughts God has placed on your heart regarding today's topic.

_____

_____

_____

_____

_____

4. Write a prayer to God.

_____

_____

_____

_____

_____

_____

Day FOUR: Surrendering to God

Practice this week's Courage Verse, Romans 8:38-39. Now try to recite it entirely from memory without glancing at your card. How did you do?

Once we genuinely see God for who He is, believe Jesus Christ bore our sins on the cross, repent and receive Christ as our personal Lord and Savior, and accept the everlasting attributes of God, we must then surrender to a daily process of becoming more Christ like.

If we want to live a more hopeful, joyful, and courageous life—in the midst of any and all circumstances—we must constantly strive to decrease the tendencies of our flesh and increase our imitation of Christ's character. Today we will discuss the fourth and final stage of how we see God, which is through our *surrender to* Him.

The word "surrender" means "to yield to the power, control, or possession of another, to give (oneself) up into the power of another especially as a prisoner."[70]

1. Describe what you believe it means to surrender your life to Christ.

_____

_____

_____

_____

_____

_____

_____

Read Philippians 2:1-13, implement the Four Basic Bible Study Steps, and record your responses and findings.

Step 1: PRAY

1. Begin by asking the Holy Spirit to guide you into all truth. Take a few minutes and write a prayer thanking God for His Word.

_____

_____

_____

_____

_____

_____

_____

---

[70] *Merriam-Webster's Collegiate Dictionary*, s. v., "surrender."

Step 2: OBSERVE

Philippians 2:1-13

1. Who is speaking and being spoken to? Who is participating in the event? _____
   _____

2. What is happening? What is being said? _____
   _____

3. When is the event or conversation taking place? _____
   _____

4. Where is the event or conversation taking place? _____
   _____

5. Why is the event or conversation taking place? _____
   _____

6. How is the event or conversation taking place?
   _____
   _____

7. Based on this passage, what does it mean to be "like Christ"?
   _____
   _____
   _____
   _____

Step 3: INTERPRET

1. What does this text mean? What Timeless Life Lesson(s) do you believe God is trying to teach us?
   _____
   _____
   _____
   _____

Step 4: APPLY

1. What do you need to do? How will you specifically apply this lesson(s) to your life?
   _____
   _____

When I think of surrendering to Christ, I think of four simple words: "Thy will be done" (Matt. 6:10 KJV).

Christ expressed this phrase three times in critical moments of His ministry: once when He gave His disciples the model for prayer and twice when He surrendered to God's will regarding His crucifixion for our salvation. Are you able to relinquish your will for God's will?

2. Explain and give examples of situations in your life where you will commit to accepting God's will, whatever the outcome.

3. Journal additional thoughts God has placed on your heart regarding today's topic.

4. Write a prayer to God.

Day FIVE: Grasping God's Love

This is your final day of lesson 9. Can you recite this week's Courage Verse, Romans 8:38-39, without looking at your card? Are you noticing any changes in your ability to memorize Scripture?

This week, we've focused on our response to God's love for us. Today, we will focus on His amazing and infinite love and consider His view of us.

Complete the second portion in Action Step 1 of chapter 14, found on page 168 in *CFL*.

1. Action Step 1b: Take an honest assessment of how you believe God sees you. Describe your view.

_____

_____

_____

On pages 161 through 163 of chapter 14 in *CFL*, I describe the four stages of how God sees us: through His creation, His love, our salvation, and our sanctification. By understanding His view, we will truly grasp His love in greater ways.

Read the following four passages, implement the Four Basic Bible Study Steps, and record your responses and findings. I have provided the Observation information to expedite your study process.

Step 1: PRAY

1. Begin by asking the Holy Spirit to guide you into all truth. Take a few minutes and write a prayer thanking God for His Word.

_____

_____

_____

_____

Step 2: OBSERVE

Genesis 1:26-31 and 2:7-8, 15-25

1. Who is speaking and being spoken to? Who is participating in the event?

    Inspired by God, Moses is describing the creation of the world and all that is in it.[71]

2. What is happening? What is being said?

    God is speaking of creating mankind, male and female (Gen. 1:26-31, 2:7-8).

---

[71] Eugene Merrill, Mark F. Rooker, and Michael A. Grisanti, *The World and the Word: An Introduction to the Old Testament* (Nashville: B&H Academic, 2011), 170-171.

3. When is the event or conversation taking place?

    N/A

4. Where is the event or conversation taking place?

    N/A

5. Why is the event or conversation taking place?

    N/A

6. How is the event or conversation taking place?

    N/A

7. Describe what this passage says about God's view of us through His eyes of creation.

    _____

    _____

    _____

    _____

    _____

    _____

John 3:16

1. Who is speaking and being spoken to? Who is participating in the event?

    Jesus is speaking to Nicodemus, a Pharisee, a ruler of the Jews (Jn. 3:1-21).

2. What is happening? What is being said?

    Nicodemus is asking Jesus questions, and Jesus is answering him (Jn. 3:1-21).

3. When is the event or conversation taking place?

    Jesus spoke to Nicodemus during His ministry to the Jews. John, an apostle of Christ, recorded the conversation sometime after Jesus' death, burial, and resurrection in the mid-AD 80s to the early-AD 90s.[72]

4. Where is the event or conversation taking place?

    In Jerusalem (Jn. 2:13).

5. Why is the event or conversation taking place?

    N/A

6. How is the event or conversation taking place?

    Jesus spoke directly to Nicodemus in the presence of His disciples. John, an eyewitness to the conversation, wrote it down.

7. Describe what this passage says about God's view of us through His eyes of love.

    _____

    _____

[72] Andreas J. Kostenberger, L. Scott Kellum, and Charles L. Quarles, *The Cradle, The Cross, And Crown: An Introduction to the New Testament* (Nashville: B&H Academic, 2016), 840, 864.

_____

_____

_____

_____

Ephesians 2:18-19

1. Who is speaking and being spoken to? Who is participating in the event?

   Paul, an Apostle of Christ, is speaking to Gentile believers in Ephesus (Eph. 1:1, 3:1).

2. What is happening? What is being said?

   Paul is discussing the importance of unity within the church; he also addresses Christian ethics and spiritual warfare.[73]

3. When is the event or conversation taking place?

   Most likely, this letter was written while Paul was imprisoned (Eph. 6:20), sometime around AD 60.[74]

4. Where is the event or conversation taking place?

   The book of Ephesians is considered a Prison Epistle (a letter written by Paul when he was in prison); most scholars believe Paul likely wrote this letter during his imprisonment in Rome.[75]

5. Why is the event or conversation taking place?

   This is a general letter to the Ephesians to help believers understand the importance of living their lives as a reflection of their relationship with Christ.[76]

6. How is the event or conversation taking place?

   According to the structure of the book of Ephesians and its historical background, Paul is communicating with believers in Ephesus by letter.

7. Describe what Scripture says about God's view of us through His eyes of our salvation.

   _____

   _____

   _____

   _____

Ephesians 4:11-16

1. Who is speaking and being spoken to? Who is participating in the event?

   Paul, an Apostle of Christ, is speaking to Gentile believers in Ephesus (Eph. 1:1, 3:1).

---

[73] Andreas J. Kostenberger, L. Scott Kellum, and Charles L. Quarles, *The Cradle, The Cross, And Crown: An Introduction to the New Testament* (Nashville: B&H Academic, 2016), 666.

[74] Ibid., 664.

[75] Ibid.

[76] Klyne Snodgrass, *The NIV Application Commentary: Ephesians* (Grand Rapids, MI: Zondervan, 1996), 44.

2. What is happening? What is being said?

   Paul is discussing the importance of unity within the church; he also addresses Christian ethics and spiritual warfare.[77]

3. When is the event or conversation taking place?

   Most likely, this letter was written while Paul was imprisoned (Eph. 6:20), sometime around AD 60.[78]

4. Where is the event or conversation taking place?

   The book of Ephesians is considered a Prison Epistle (a letter written by Paul when he was in prison); most scholars believe Paul likely wrote this letter during his imprisonment in Rome.[79]

5. Why is the event or conversation taking place?

   This is a general letter to the Ephesians to help believers understand the importance of living their lives as a reflection of their relationship with Christ.[80]

6. How is the event or conversation taking place?

   According to the structure of the book of Ephesians and its historical background, Paul is communicating with believers in Ephesus by letter.

7. Describe what Scripture says about God's view of us through His eyes of our sanctification.

   _____

   _____

   _____

   _____

   _____

Step 3: INTERPRET

1. What do these texts mean? What Timeless Life Lessons do you believe God is trying to teach us in these passages?

   Genesis 1:26-31 and 2:7-8, 15-25

   _____

   _____

   _____

   _____

---

[77] Andreas J. Kostenberger, L. Scott Kellum, and Charles L. Quarles, *The Cradle, The Cross, And Crown: An Introduction to the New Testament* (Nashville: B&H Academic, 2016), 666.

[78] Ibid., 664.

[79] Ibid.

[80] Klyne Snodgrass, *The NIV Application Commentary: Ephesians* (Grand Rapids, MI: Zondervan, 1996), 44.

John 3:16

_____

_____

_____

_____

Ephesians 2:18-19

_____

_____

_____

_____

Ephesians 4:11-16

_____

_____

_____

_____

Step 4: APPLY

1. What do you need to do? How will you specifically apply these lessons to your life?

_____

_____

_____

_____

Complete Action Step 2 of chapter 14, found on page 168 in _CFL._

2. Action Step 2: Describe the stage you believe you are in on your spiritual growth journey: seeing, believing, accepting, or surrendering. Write out what stage you would like to see yourself grow into. Pray about the importance of studying God's Word and write down a challenge you are willing to take to improve your knowledge and understanding of Scripture.

_____

_____

_____

_____

_____

_____

_____

_____

_____

_____

3. Journal additional thoughts God has placed on your heart regarding today's topic.

_____

_____

_____

_____

_____

4. Write out a prayer to God.

_____

_____

_____

_____

_____

I applaud you for how far you've come! You've just completed lesson 9, and you're in the home stretch. I pray you're feeling good about the progress you're making. You're only one step away from completing your seventh COURAGE step and just three lessons away from our courageous journey finish line.

As we move on to lesson 10, "Embrace a Life of Grace," and begin step 7, let's review and apply our Courage Quote, Courage Verse, and Timeless Life Lessons from this week's study and take some time to truly celebrate and give thanks for God's unfathomable love for us.

REVIEW

COURAGE QUOTE

We all desire a love that is unconditional, available, consistent, and everlasting. God's love is all of the above and so much more—if we choose to embrace it.

COURAGE VERSE

For I am convinced that neither death, nor life, nor angels, nor principalities, nor things present, nor things to come, nor powers, nor height, nor depth, nor any other created thing, will be able to separate us from the love of God, which is in Christ Jesus our Lord.

–Romans 8:38-39

Timeless Life Lessons Learned

_____

_____

_____

_____

_____

_____

_____

_____

_____

_____

E STEP IN COURAGE

EMBRACE A LIFE OF GRACE

COURAGE QUOTE

Grace extends endless chances, doesn't keep score, and refuses to rejoice when mistakes are made.

COURAGE VERSE

And He has said to me, "My grace is sufficient for you, for power is perfected in weakness."
Most gladly, therefore, I will rather boast about my weaknesses,
so that the power of Christ may dwell in me.

—2 Corinthians 12:9

The doctrine of grace sets Christianity apart from every other religion in the world.[81] "Grace is practically a synonym for *SALVATION*."[82] It can be defined as giving to someone, not to get, but simply to help the other person.[83]

Over the past nine weeks, we have prepared for and walked through six of our seven COURAGE Steps. This week, we will complete step 7 by analyzing our capacity to fully embrace God's amazing grace and by evaluating our ability to give and receive grace.

Day ONE: Understanding Grace

Write this week's Courage Verse, 2 Corinthians 12:9, on a note card. Place it where you will see it often and practice memorizing it throughout the week.

Read Chapter 15 in *CFL*, "Embrace a Life of Grace."

---

[81] Charles C. Ryrie, *The Grace of God* (Chicago: Moody Press, 1963), 10-11.

[82] Moisés Silva and Merrill Chapin Tenney, *The Zondervan Encyclopedia of the Bible, D-G* (Grand Rapids, MI: The Zondervan Corporation, 2009), 840.

[83] Ibid.

1. The Bible is full of verses about God's unending love and amazing grace. Write the following verses, take a few minutes to pray over each one, and thank God for our undeserved gift of grace.

   Ephesians 2:8-9

   _____

   _____

   _____

   Romans 6:14

   _____

   _____

   _____

   Hebrews 4:16

   _____

   _____

   _____

   James 4:6

   _____

   _____

   _____

   Complete Action Step 1 of chapter 15, found on page 180 in *CFL*.

2. Action Step 1: Write a paragraph about what embracing God's grace means to you.

   _____

   _____

   _____

   _____

   _____

3. Journal additional thoughts God has placed on your heart regarding today's topic.

   _____

   _____

4. Write a prayer to God.

Day TWO: Experiencing Grace

Practice this week's Courage Verse, 2 Corinthians 12:9.

Read 2 Samuel chapters 11 through 12:23, implement the Four Basic Bible Study Steps, and record your responses and findings.

Step 1: PRAY

1. Begin by asking the Holy Spirit to guide you into all truth. Take a few minutes and write a prayer thanking God for His Word.

Step 2: OBSERVE

2 Samuel 11-12:23

1. Who is speaking and being spoken to? Who is participating in the event? _____

_____

2. What is happening? What is being said? _____

_____

3. When is the event or conversation taking place? _____

_____

4. Where is the event or conversation taking place? _____

_____

5. Why is the event or conversation taking place? _____

_____

6. How is the event or conversation taking place?

_____

_____

7. Describe what you learned about King David's sin.

_____

_____

_____

_____

8. Describe how God approached David regarding his sin.

_____

_____

_____

_____

9. Describe David's repentance, God's grace, the consequences for David's sin, and David's reaction once he received the news that his son had died.

_____

_____

_____

_____

10. Write the following verses and compare them to 2 Samuel 11:12-23. Describe what you learn about God's grace toward David.

    1 Kings 3:6

_____

_____

_____

_____

2 Chronicles 1:8

Step 3: INTERPRET

1. What does this text mean? What Timeless Life Lesson(s) do you believe God is trying to teach us in these passages?

Step 4: APPLY

1. What do you need to do? How will you specifically apply this lesson(s) to your life?

2. Journal additional thoughts God has placed on your heart regarding today's topic.

3. Write a prayer to God.

_____

_____

_____

Day THREE: Grasping Grace

Practice this week's Courage Verse, 2 Corinthians 12:9. Are you able to recite it without looking at your card? Try it and see.

Read chapter 5 in Romans, implement the Four Basic Bible Study Steps, and record your responses and findings.

Step 1: PRAY

1. Begin by asking the Holy Spirit to guide you into all truth. Take a few minutes and write a prayer thanking God for His Word.

_____

_____

_____

_____

Step 2: OBSERVE

Romans 5

1. Who is speaking and being spoken to? Who is participating in the event? _____

    _____

2. What is happening? What is being said? _____

    _____

3. When is the event or conversation taking place? _____

    _____

4. Where is the event or conversation taking place? _____

    _____

5. Why is the event or conversation taking place? _____

    _____

6. How is the event or conversation taking place?

    _____

7. Describe what you learn from this chapter about the following topics.

    The character of God

    _____

    _____

    _____

    _____

    _____

    _____

    The character of man

    _____

    _____

    _____

    _____

    _____

    _____

    Gifts we receive through Christ

    _____

    _____

    _____

    _____

    _____

    _____

    Grace

    _____

    _____

    _____

    _____

    _____

    _____

    _____

Step 3: INTERPRET

1. What does this text mean? What Timeless Life Lesson(s) do you believe God is trying to teach us?

Step 4: APPLY

1. What do you need to do? How will you specifically apply this lesson(s) to your life?

2. Journal additional thoughts God has placed on your heart regarding today's topic.

3. Write a prayer to God.

Day FOUR: Giving Grace

Practice this week's Courage Verse, 2 Corinthians 12:9. Now try to recite it entirely from memory, without glancing at your card. I wish I could be there to hear you. I'll bet your doing great!

Numerous accounts in the Bible tell of godly men and women extending grace to people who had mistreated them. One of the most notable accounts being that of Joseph, in the book of Genesis. We studied the biblical account of Joseph's life in lesson 4, but it bears another look with regards to his willingness to extend grace to his brothers.

Review your study of Joseph on day 4 of lesson 4, "Recognizing Circumstances and Coping Skills." Before you do, be sure to exercise our first Basic Bible Study Step: Pray.

Step 1: PRAY

1. Begin by asking the Holy Spirit to guide you into all truth. Take a few minutes and write a prayer thanking God for His Word.

_____

_____

_____

_____

Step 2: OBSERVE

1. Consulting Genesis chapter 37, describe Joseph's relationship with his brothers.

_____

_____

_____

_____

_____

_____

Genesis chapters 38 through 41 recount a large portion of Joseph's life in Egypt as a slave and prisoner. Throughout each situation Joseph faced, he consistently remained faithful to God and was continually blessed by God. Eventually, Joseph was promoted to ruler over all Egypt by Pharaoh himself, a position that brought to life Joseph's childhood dreams. Genesis 42:1-26 gives the account of Joseph's brothers' trip to Egypt.

2. Write a brief description of their visit.

_____

_____

_____

_____

_____

_____

_____

3. Genesis 45:1-15 gives an account of Joseph's grace-filled response toward his brothers.

   Write a brief description of his gracious response.

_____

_____

_____

_____

_____

_____

_____

Now, let's complete the final two Basic Bible Study Steps, Interpret and Apply, as they relate to God's grace.

Step 3: INTERPRET

1. What does this text mean? What Timeless Life Lesson(s) do you believe God is trying to teach us?

_____

_____

_____

_____

Step 4: APPLY

1. What do you need to do? How will you specifically apply this lesson(s) to your life?

_____

_____

_____

2. Journal additional thoughts God has placed on your heart regarding today's topic.

_____

_____

_____

_____

_____

_____

_____

_____

_____

3. Write a prayer to God.

_____

_____

_____

_____

_____

_____

_____

_____

_____

_____

Day FIVE: Grace in Action

This is the final day of lesson 10. Can you recite this week's Courage Verse, 2 Corinthians 12:9, without looking at your card? I have no doubt you're getting good at these memorization exercises.

We've worked diligently this week to understand and embrace grace. So far, we've discussed the true meaning of grace, what it means to fully grasp and receive grace, and how important it is for us to extend grace to others. Let's take time today to reflect on areas of our lives where God is encouraging us to take action, in grace.

Complete Action Step 2, found on page 180 in *CFL*.

Action Step 2: Ask God to reveal trigger situations in your life where your ability to extend grace is often tested. We discussed emotional triggers in chapter 8 in *CFL*, "Ten Common Obstacles," part of the *O* Step in COURAGE. You may want to review this information on page 89 in *CFL* to refresh your memory.

1. Write about the trigger situations in which your ability to extend grace is tested. Ask God to reveal people in your life who need to receive grace from you. Write down their names and at least one way you could extend grace to them. Then pray for each one.

_____

_____

_____

_____

_____

_____

_____

2. Journal additional thoughts God has placed on your heart regarding today's topic.

_____

_____

_____

_____

_____

_____

_____

3. Write a prayer to God.

_____

_____

_____

_____

_____

_____

_____

Today is a very special day—you've completed lesson 10 and all seven COURAGE steps. Bravo! You've studied passages that help you understand grace, and you have courageously considered what God is specifically calling you to do in the area of giving and receiving grace freely.

As we move on to lesson 11, "Move Forward in Freedom," let's review and apply our Courage Quote, Courage Verse, and Timeless Life Lessons from this week's study. By fully embracing grace, you prepare yourself to courageously pursue a life of freedom.

LESSON 10

REVIEW

COURAGE QUOTE

Grace extends endless chances, doesn't keep score, and refuses to rejoice when mistakes are made.

COURAGE VERSE

And He has said to me, "My grace is sufficient for you, for power is perfected in weakness." Most gladly, therefore, I will rather boast about my weaknesses, so that the power of Christ may dwell in me.

–2 Corinthians 12:9

Timeless Life Lessons Learned

_____

_____

_____

_____

_____

_____

_____

_____

_____

_____

MOVE FORWARD IN FREEDOM

Freedom gives us the opportunity to employ our God-given gifts
and pursue our God-given dreams.

It was for freedom that Christ set us free;
therefore keep standing firm and do not be subject again to a yoke of slavery.

–Galatians 5:1

As you study the final two chapters of *CFL*, it's time to take an honest inventory of the progress you've made over the past ten weeks and determine the necessary steps you still need to take toward courage. You've made commitments to change, identified your obstacles, and started breaking them down. You've uncovered your true identity, learned to embrace who God created you to be, and replaced worldly lies with scriptural truth. You've learned to accept the things you cannot change and to change the things you can. And last, but certainly not least, you've focused on grasping the magnitude of God's love and embracing His free gift of grace.

During this week's lesson, we will focus on five critical components that allow us to fully usher in our newfound freedom. On page 182 of chapter 16 in *CFL*, I mention five additional steps we can take to remove any lingering restraints as we move forward in freedom. Over the next five days, we will consider biblical accounts that encourage us to courageously implement each of these additional steps: resist Satan, extend forgiveness, grow friendships, improve communication, and develop perseverance.

Day ONE: Resist Satan

Write this week's Courage Verse, Galatians 5:1, on a note card. Place it where you will see it often and practice memorizing it throughout the week.

Read chapter 16 in *CFL*, "Move Forward in Freedom."

Now, read Mathew 4:1-11, implement the Four Basic Bible Study Steps, and record your responses and findings. I have provided the Observation information to expedite your study process.

Step 1: PRAY

1. Begin by asking the Holy Spirit to guide you into all truth. Take a few minutes and write a prayer thanking God for His Word.

_____

_____

_____

_____

Step 2: OBSERVE

Mathew 4:1-11

1. Who is speaking and being spoken to? Who is participating in the event?

   Matthew, an apostle of Christ and eyewitness to the life of Christ, is recording this historical account for believers.[84] *In this account of Jesus' life, Jesus and Satan are communicating (Matt. 4:1-11).*

2. What is happening? What is being said?

   Satan tempted Jesus with food, pride, and authority (Matt. 4:3, 5-6, 8-9), and Jesus answered Satan by quoting Scripture (Matt. 4:4, 7, 10).

3. When is the event or conversation taking place?

   After Christ was baptized (Matt. 3:13-17) and just before He began His preaching/teaching ministry (Matt. 4:17).

4. Where is the event or conversation taking place?

   In the wilderness (Matt. 4:1).

5. Why is the event or conversation taking place?

   To strengthen and prepare Jesus for the ministry for which He was born.[85]

6. How is the event or conversation taking place?

   N/A

7. Describe how Jesus resisted temptation.

   _____

   _____

   _____

---

[84] Andreas J. Kostenberger, L. Scott Kellum, and Charles L. Quarles, *The Cradle, The Cross, And Crown: An Introduction to the New Testament* (Nashville: B&H Academic, 2016), 226.

[85] Michael J. Wilkins, *The NIV Application Commentary: Matthew* (Grand Rapids, MI: Zondervan Publishing House, 2004), 155.

8. To put Matthew 4:1-11 in context, read Matthew 3:13-17 and 4:12-17. Briefly describe the events that took place just before and just after Jesus' temptation.

9. Explain what you believe to be the significance of the sequence of the three events described in Matthew 3:13 through 4:17.

Step 3: INTERPRET

1. What does this text mean? What Timeless Life Lesson(s) do you believe God is trying to teach us?

Step 4: APPLY

1. What do you need to do? How will you specifically apply this lesson(s) to your life?

2. Describe areas of your life in which you need to resist Satan.

_____

_____

_____

_____

3. Journal additional thoughts God has placed on your heart regarding today's topic.

_____

_____

_____

_____

_____

_____

_____

4. Write a prayer to God.

_____

_____

_____

_____

_____

_____

_____

_____

Day TWO: Extend Forgiveness

Practice this week's Courage Verse, Galatians 5:1.

Once we surrender our life to Christ, we embark on a sanctification journey for the rest of our lives, in which we strive to become more like Christ (cf. Col. 3:1-25).

As we move forward in freedom and work to remove and/or manage lingering obstacles, we must look to Christ, our ultimate role model, for guidance. So, let's look at a biblical account that reveals Christ's character and consider the way He dealt with temptation, forgiveness, and friendships.

Read Luke 7:44-50, implement the Four Basic Bible Study Steps, and record your responses and findings.

Step 1: PRAY

1. Begin by asking the Holy Spirit to guide you into all truth. Take a few minutes and write a prayer thanking God for His Word.

_____

_____

_____

_____

Step 2: OBSERVE

Luke 7:44-50

1. Who is speaking and being spoken to? Who is participating in the event? _____

_____

2. What is happening? What is being said? _____

_____

3. When is the event or conversation taking place? _____

_____

4. Where is the event or conversation taking place? _____

_____

5. Why is the event or conversation taking place? _____

_____

6. How is the event or conversation taking place?

_____

_____

7. Describe how Jesus displays and views forgiveness.

_____

_____

_____

_____

Step 3: INTERPRET

1. What does this text mean? What Timeless Life Lesson(s) do you believe God is trying to teach us?

_____

_____

Step 4: APPLY

1. What do you need to do? How will you specifically apply this lesson(s) to your life?

2. Describe areas of your life in which you need to extend forgiveness.

3. Journal additional thoughts God has placed on your heart regarding today's topic.

4. Write a prayer to God.

Day THREE: Grow Friendships

Practice this week's Courage Verse, Galatians 5:1. Are you able to recite any of it without looking at your card? Try it and see.

When Christ began His ministry on earth, His first task was to invite twelve men to become His friends, confidants, mentees, and ministry companions. In essence, He was the first "life coach" to ever walk the earth.

Read John 15:12-17, implement the Four Basic Bible Study Steps, and record your responses and findings.

Step 1: PRAY

1. Begin by asking the Holy Spirit to guide you into all truth. Take a few minutes and write a prayer thanking God for His Word.

_____

_____

_____

_____

_____

Step 2: OBSERVE

John 15:12-17

1. Who is speaking and being spoken to? Who is participating in the event? _____

   _____

2. What is happening? What is being said? _____

   _____

3. When is the event or conversation taking place? _____

   _____

4. Where is the event or conversation taking place? _____

   _____

5. Why is the event or conversation taking place? _____

   _____

6. How is the event or conversation taking place?

   _____

   _____

7. Explain how Jesus views His relationship with His disciples and how He desires for them to relate to one another.

_____

_____

_____

_____

_____

Step 3: INTERPRET

1. What does this text mean? What Timeless Life Lesson(s) do you believe God is trying to teach us?

_____

_____

_____

_____

_____

Step 4: APPLY

1. What do you need to do? How will you specifically apply this lesson(s) to your life?

_____

_____

_____

2. Describe areas of your life in which you need to grow friendships.

_____

_____

_____

3. Journal additional thoughts God has placed on your heart regarding today's topic.

_____

_____

_____

_____

_____

_____

_____

4. Write a prayer to God.

_____

_____

_____

_____

_____

_____

_____

Day FOUR: Improve Communication

Over the past three days, we've studied biblical accounts that reveal Christ's character and ways He dealt with temptation, forgiveness, and friendships. Today and tomorrow, we will look at biblical accounts that reveal Christ's character and how He dealt with communication and perseverance.

After inviting His disciples to follow Him, Jesus spent an extensive amount of time "doing life" with them. He exercised great patience with His followers and gave them a great deal of time and attention. When it came to communication, Jesus expressed Himself in ways that magnified the truth in love. He taught with ultimate authority and never hesitated to confront when necessary, all while opposing sinners with careful considera-tion and compassion. Wouldn't it be an amazing thing if we could all respond to the people in our lives with such compassion?

Read Mark 7:1-8, 8:13-21 and John 8:1-11, 13:1-8. Implement the Four Basic Bible Study Steps and record your responses and findings. I have provided the Observation information to expedite your study process.

Step 1: PRAY

1. Begin by asking the Holy Spirit to guide you into all truth. Take a few minutes and write a prayer thanking God for His Word.

_____

_____

_____

_____

Step 2: OBSERVE

Mark 7:1-8

1. Who is speaking and being spoken to? Who is participating in the event?

   Mark, who was believed to have been closely associated with Simon Peter (disciple of Christ and eyewitness to Jesus' ministry), is recording this historical account for believers.[86] *In this account of Jesus' life, Jesus and Satan are communicating (Mk. 4:1-11).*

2. What is happening? What is being said?

   Jesus is answering a question posed by the Pharisees and scribes, regarding His disciples eating without properly cleaning their hands (Mk. 7:1-13).

3. When is the event or conversation taking place?

   Sometime after feeding five thousand followers (Mk. 6:34-44) and walking on water (Mk. 6:47-50); before and after healing the sick (Mk. 6:54-56, 7:25-35).

4. Where is the event or conversation taking place?

   Gennesaret, northwest countryside of the Sea of Galilee (Mk. 6:53).[87]

5. Why is the event or conversation taking place?

   N/A

6. How is the event or conversation taking place?

   N/A

Step 3: INTERPRET

1. What does this text mean? What Timeless Life Lesson(s) do you believe God is trying to teach us?

   _____

   _____

   _____

   _____

2. Describe how Jesus communicated with the Pharisees.

   _____

   _____

   _____

   _____

---

[86] Andreas J. Kostenberger, L. Scott Kellum, and Charles L. Quarles, *The Cradle, The Cross, And Crown: An Introduction to the New Testament* (Nashville: B&H Academic, 2016), 276-280.

[87] Spiros Zodhiates, *The Complete Word Study Dictionary: New Testament* (Chattanooga: AMG Publishers, 2000).

Step 2: OBSERVE

Mark 8:13-21

1. Who is speaking and being spoken to? Who is participating in the event?

    Mark, who was believed to have been closely associated with Simon Peter (disciple of Christ and eyewitness to Jesus' ministry), is recording this historical account for believers.[88] In this account of Jesus' life, Jesus and Satan are communicating (Mk. 4:1-11).

2. What is happening? What is being said?

    Jesus is questioning His disciples' faith in who He is and in His ability to provide for their needs (Mk. 8:17-18).

3. When is the event or conversation taking place?

    Shortly after feeding four thousand followers (Mk. 8:5-9) and being challenged by the Pharisees to give them a sign from heaven; before healing the blind man at Bethsaida (Mk. 8:22-25).

4. Where is the event or conversation taking place?

    The east side of the Sea of Galilee, across from Dalmanutha (Mk. 8:10, 13).

5. Why is the event or conversation taking place?

    Jesus seized every opportunity to teach His disciples.

6. How is the event or conversation taking place?

    N/A

Step 3: INTERPRET

1. What does this text mean? What Timeless Life Lesson(s) do you believe God is trying to teach us?

    _____

    _____

    _____

    _____

2. Describe how Jesus communicated with His disciples.

    _____

    _____

    _____

    _____

---

[88] Andreas J. Kostenberger, L. Scott Kellum, and Charles L. Quarles, *The Cradle, The Cross, And Crown: An Introduction to the New Testament* (Nashville: B&H Academic, 2016), 276-280.

Step 2: OBSERVE

John 8:1-11

1. Who is speaking and being spoken to? Who is participating in the event?

    Jesus is speaking to the scribes and Pharisees (Jn. 8:3-4, 7).

2. What is happening? What is being said?

    The scribes and Pharisees brought a woman caught in adultery to Jesus and asked Him if He believed they should stone her to death (Jn. 8:3-5).

3. When is the event or conversation taking place?

    As Jesus is teaching the people in the temple (Jn. 8:2).

4. Where is the event or conversation taking place?

    At the Mount of Olives, in the center of the court of the temple (Mk. 8:1-3).

5. Why is the event or conversation taking place?

    The scribes and Pharisees wanted to test Jesus, "so that they might have grounds to accuse Him" (Jn. 8:6).

6. How is the event or conversation taking place?

    N/A

Step 3: INTERPRET

1. What does this text mean? What Timeless Life Lesson(s) do you believe God is trying to teach us?

    _____

    _____

    _____

    _____

2. Describe how Jesus communicated with the Pharisees and with the woman caught in adultery.

    _____

    _____

    _____

    _____

    _____

Step 2: OBSERVE

John 13:1-8

1. Who is speaking and being spoken to? Who is participating in the event?

    Jesus and His disciples (Jn. 13:5).

2. What is happening? What is being said?

   Jesus got up from supper and washed His disciples' feet (Jn. 13:4-5). Simon Peter questioned Jesus as to why He was doing this (Jn. 13:6).

3. When is the event or conversation taking place?

   Shortly before the Feast of Passover (Jn. 13:1) and before being arrested (Jn. 18:12), accused, beaten (Jn. 19:1-3), and crucified (Jn. 19:17-18).

4. Where is the event or conversation taking place?

   In the home of a man from Jerusalem, in a large upper room (Matt. 26:17-19; Mk. 14:12-16; Lk. 22:8-13).

5. Why is the event or conversation taking place?

   Jesus wanted to give His disciples an example for them to follow (Jn. 13:15).

6. How is the event or conversation taking place?

   N/A

Step 3: INTERPRET

1. What does this text mean? What Timeless Life Lesson(s) do you believe God is trying to teach us?

   _____

   _____

   _____

   _____

2. Describe how Jesus communicated with His disciples.

   _____

   _____

   _____

   _____

Step 4: APPLY

1. What do you need to do? How will you specifically apply the lessons from Mark 7, 8 and John 8, 13 to your life?

   _____

   _____

   _____

   _____

2. Journal additional thoughts God has placed on your heart regarding today's topic.

_____

_____

_____

_____

_____

_____

_____

3. Write a prayer to God.

_____

_____

_____

_____

_____

_____

_____

_____

Day FIVE: Develop Perseverance

This is your final day of lesson 11, and I'm not even going to ask if you can recite this week's Courage Verse without looking at your card. I'm sure you can!

Read Luke 18:1-8, implement the Four Basic Bible Study Steps, and record your responses and findings.

Step 1: PRAY

1. Begin by asking the Holy Spirit to guide you into all truth. Take a few minutes and write a prayer thanking God for His Word.

_____

_____

_____

_____

Step 2: OBSERVE

Luke 18:1-8

1. Who is speaking and being spoken to? Who is participating in the event? _____

2. What is happening? What is being said? _____

3. When is the event or conversation taking place? _____

4. Where is the event or conversation taking place? _____

5. Why is the event or conversation taking place? _____

6. How is the event or conversation taking place?

7. Describe what Jesus taught about perseverance.

Step 3: INTERPRET

1. What does this text mean? What Timeless Life Lesson(s) do you believe God is trying to teach us?

Step 4: APPLY

1. What do you need to do? How will you specifically apply this lesson(s) to your life?

_____

_____

_____

_____

_____

Complete Action Steps 1 and 2 of chapter 16, found on page 193.

2. Action Step 1: Take a moment to pray about circumstances where you are in need of God's empowerment to help you resist Satan, extend forgiveness, grow friendships, improve communication, or persevere. Ask God to use your life circumstances to develop these areas in your life and ultimately bring Him glory.

3. Action Step 2: Write down at least one goal for each of the five steps for moving forward in freedom: resist Satan, extend forgiveness, grow friendships, improve communication, and develop perseverance. Develop a plan to implement these goals in the coming week and take action.

Resist Satan:

_____

_____

Extend Forgiveness:

_____

_____

Grow Friendships:

_____

_____

Improve Communication:

_____

_____

Develop Perseverance:

_____

_____

_____

4. Journal additional thoughts God has placed on your heart regarding today's topic.

_____

_____

_____

_____

_____

_____

_____

5. Write a prayer to God.

_____

_____

_____

_____

_____

_____

_____

Once again, hearty congratulations are in order! You've completed lesson 11 and studied specific passages that urge you to resist temptation, extend forgiveness, grow friendships, improve communication, and develop perseverance.

As we move on to our final lesson, "Find Joy in the Journey," let's review and apply our Courage Quote, Courage Verse, and Timeless Life Lessons from this week's study. By exercising this week's five important steps, we fortify our foundation of courage and free ourselves from any lingering obstacles. Are you beginning to feel a weight lifting from your shoulders? If so, that's what courage feels like!

LESSON 11

REVIEW

COURAGE QUOTE

Freedom gives us the opportunity to employ our God-given gifts
and pursue our God-given dreams.

COURAGE VERSE

It was for freedom that Christ set us free;
therefore keep standing firm and do not be subject again to a yoke of slavery.

–Galatians 5:1

Timeless Life Lessons Learned

_____

_____

_____

_____

_____

_____

_____

_____

_____

_____

_____

_____

FIND JOY IN THE JOURNEY

True joy is a product of comfort in the midst of crisis, trust in the midst of uncertainty, and hope in the midst of all circumstances.

Now may the God of hope fill you with all joy and peace in believing, so that you will abound in hope by the power of the Holy Spirit.

–Romans 15:13

Somehow, "congratulations" just doesn't sound like enough for all you've accomplished over the past twelve weeks. Bravo and to God be the glory for all you've done! You've taken this long journey through seven steps of COURAGE and have persevered through exercises that have challenged you to make difficult changes. You have embraced life with new-found freedom and found abundant courage. Now, it's time to add the final ingredient to our recipe. Consider it the icing on the cake, the secret sauce, the critical component that is needed to embrace life as a newly discovered adventure.

While it takes courage to overcome challenges, endure difficult seasons, and embrace new life, it is *joy* that brings a smile to our face, warmth to our heart, and get-up-and-go to our everyday life. And it's important to remember, dear sojourner, joy is a *choice*.

You've worked hard to overcome the barriers preventing you from moving forward in freedom. Now, let's discuss how you can maintain an optimistic outlook regarding your circumstances while you courageously pursue life. This week we're going to discuss five ways we can magnify the joy in our lives.

Day ONE: Positive Perspectives

Write this week's Courage Verse on a note card and add it as the last precious piece to your courage puzzle—the final note card in a collection of memory verses that I encourage you to keep and refer to often. Have you noticed over the course of your study how often a verse will pop into your mind at just the right moment?

Memorizing Scripture is a valuable tool, not only in strengthening your courage muscles but also in strengthening your relationship with God.

As you've no doubt gathered by now, courage is a choice that involves actions and decisions that are sometimes difficult and often provoke a struggle. It's important for us to keep a positive perspective as we exercise our new-found courage and keep our eyes on God, His blessings, and His promises for our future.

Read chapter 17 in *CFL*, "Find Joy in the Journey."

Read Philippians 4:6-9, implement the Four Basic Bible Study Steps, and record your responses and findings. And, for our final time together in this study, I have once again provided the Observation information to expedite your study process.

Step 1: PRAY

1. Begin by asking the Holy Spirit to guide you into all truth. Take a few minutes and write a prayer thanking God for His Word.

_____

_____

_____

_____

Step 2: OBSERVE

Philippians 4:6-9

1. Who is speaking and being spoken to? Who is participating in the event?

    Paul, a bond-servant of Christ, is speaking to believers, including overseers and deacons, in Philippi (Phil. 1:1).

2. What is happening? What is being said?

    Paul urges believers to live in harmony and have the same attitude as Christ (Phil. 2:1-5). He warns them to disregard lessons taught by false teachers (Phil. 3:2), and he addresses issues caused by two women in the church, Euodia and Syntyche (Phil. 4:2-3).

3. When is the event or conversation taking place?

    Likely sometime between AD 50 and AD 63.[89]

4. Where is the event or conversation taking place?

    Philippians is considered a Prison Epistle; most scholars believe Paul likely wrote this letter during his imprisonment in Rome (Phil. 1:12-13).[90]

---

[89] Andreas J. Kostenberger, Scott Kellum, and Charles L. Quarles, *The Cradle, The Cross, And Crown: An Introduction to the New Testament* (Nashville: B&H Academic, 2016), 641.

[90] Ibid., 644-645.

5. Why is the event or conversation taking place?

   Paul wanted to encourage believers to partner with one another in the gospel and live a life worthy of Christ's sacrifice.[91]

6. How is the event or conversation taking place?

   Paul is communicating with believers in Philippi by means of a letter (Phil. 3:3).

7. Describe what you learn about positive thinking.

   _____

   _____

   _____

   _____

   _____

   _____

Step 3: INTERPRET

1. What does this text mean? What Timeless Life Lesson(s) do you believe God is trying to teach us?

   _____

   _____

   _____

   _____

Step 4: APPLY

1. What do you need to do? How will you specifically apply this lesson(s) to your life?

   _____

   _____

   _____

   _____

2. Write your commitment to maintain a positive perspective—regardless of past, present, or future circumstances.

   _____

   _____

   _____

   _____

   _____

---

[91] Ibid., 646.

_____

_____

3. Journal additional thoughts God has placed on your heart regarding today's topic.

_____

_____

_____

_____

_____

_____

_____

4. Write a prayer to God.

_____

_____

_____

_____

_____

_____

_____

Day TWO: An Attitude of Gratitude

Practice this week's Courage Verse, Romans 15:13.

We have so much to be thankful for, yet many times we allow the demands of life and the struggles we face to overshadow our blessings. Life can be difficult, discouraging, and even painful at times, but God is ever-present, always working in the background of our situations to lead us toward a path of hope, healing, and restoration.

No matter what situation or circumstance we find ourselves in, we can choose to focus on our blessings rather than our worries and to be grateful for areas of our lives where we do experience enjoyment and success. When we choose a heart of gratitude, we realize hope and experience joy that can only be found in our relationship with God.

Let's take time today to consider areas of our lives where we experience joy and success. Complete Action Step 1 of chapter 17, found on page 204 in *CFL*.

1. Read Colossians 3:15-17, implement the Four Basic Bible Study Steps, and record your responses and findings.

2. Action Step 1: Write down at least five things you are thankful for. Praise God for them and let them be the foundation of your joy throughout each day. (Consider doing this from now on. You will be amazed at the difference it will make in your perspective.)

_____

_____

_____

_____

_____

_____

Step 1: PRAY

1. Begin by asking the Holy Spirit to guide you into all truth. Take a few minutes and write a prayer thanking God for His Word.

_____

_____

_____

_____

Step 2: OBSERVE

Colossians 3:15-17

1. Who is speaking and being spoken to? Who is participating in the event? _____

_____

2. What is happening? What is being said? _____

_____

3. When is the event or conversation taking place? _____

_____

4. Where is the event or conversation taking place? _____

_____

5. Why is the event or conversation taking place? _____

_____

6. How is the event or conversation taking place? _____

_____

7. Describe what you learned from this passage about God's involvement in your dreams and purposes.

_____

_____

_____

_____

_____

_____

Step 3: INTERPRET

1. What does this text mean? What Timeless Life Lesson(s) do you believe God is trying to teach us?

_____

_____

_____

_____

Step 4: APPLY

1. What do you need to do? How will you specifically apply this lesson(s) to your life?

_____

_____

_____

_____

2. Write your commitment to maintain an attitude of thankfulness.

_____

_____

_____

_____

_____

_____

3. Journal additional thoughts God has placed on your heart regarding today's topic.

_____

_____

_____

_____

_____

_____

_____

4. Write a prayer to God.

_____

_____

_____

_____

_____

_____

_____

Day THREE: Daring to Dream

Practice this week's Courage Verse, Romans 15:13, and praise God for the memory muscles He has given you over the past weeks.

As you come to the end of this study, it's time to consider the dreams God has given you and exercise your new-found courage to pursue those dreams. There's nothing standing in your way!

1. Take five to ten minutes and consider your dreams. Write them down, pray over them, and ask God to reveal His dreams and purpose for you.

_____

_____

_____

_____

_____

_____

_____

_____

_____

Read Hebrews 13:20-21, implement the Four Basic Bible Study Steps, and record your responses and findings.

Step 1: PRAY

1. Begin by asking the Holy Spirit to guide you into all truth. Take a few minutes and write a prayer thanking God for His Word.

_____

_____

_____

_____

Step 2: OBSERVE

Hebrews 13:20-21

1. Who is speaking and being spoken to? Who is participating in the event? _____

_____

2. What is happening? What is being said? _____

_____

3. When is the event or conversation taking place? _____

_____

4. Where is the event or conversation taking place? _____

_____

5. Why is the event or conversation taking place? _____

_____

6. How is the event or conversation taking place?

_____

_____

7. Describe what you learned from this passage about God's involvement in your dreams and purposes.

_____

_____

_____

_____

Step 3: INTERPRET

1. What does this text mean? What Timeless Life Lesson(s) do you believe God is trying to teach us?

_____

_____

_____

_____

Step 4: APPLY

1. What do you need to do? How will you specifically apply this lesson(s) to your life?

_____

_____

_____

_____

2. Journal additional thoughts God has placed on your heart regarding today's life-changing topic.

_____

_____

_____

_____

_____

_____

3. Write a prayer to God.

_____

_____

_____

_____

_____

_____

Day FOUR: Setting Goals

As you practice this final Courage Verse, think back to week 1 when the habit was new. Chances are good that it was difficult for you back then. Am I right? However, if you've been completing all these memory verse assignments over the past weeks, I can almost guarantee that it's getting easier for you to recite verses without reading your note card. The mind is a muscle that needs exercising, just like the rest of our body, and the more you challenge it to recall things, the better it gets at doing so. Right?

Take the next ten to fifteen minutes and ask God to make known _how_ He desires for you to accomplish your God-given dreams.

1. Write goals on how you intend to courageously pursue these dreams.

_____

_____

_____

_____

_____

As you pursue your dreams and God-given purpose, you will need to consistently draw from God's reservoir of courage. Throughout this study, we have exercised our courage muscles, preparing ourselves to set aside fears and take bold, courageous steps forward.

2. Describe ways you have implemented your new-found courage over the past twelve weeks of this study. What are the most significant changes you see in your life?

_____

_____

_____

_____

_____

Complete Action Step 2 of chapter 17, found on page 204 in *CFL*.

3. Action Step 2: Write your goals for implementing the seven COURAGE steps into your daily life and pursuing your God-given dreams.

_____

_____

_____

_____

_____

_____

_____

_____

4. Journal additional thoughts God has placed on your heart regarding today's topic.

_____

_____

_____

_____

_____

_____

5. Write a prayer to God.

_____

_____

_____

_____

_____

_____

_____

_____

Day FIVE: Take Action

Okay, my courageous friend, this is the last time we'll be together on our journey—the last time I'm going to ask you to recite our Courage Verse, Romans 15:13, and I know you can do it without looking at your card. Great job! Remember, save these Scripture "flash cards" and refer to them often.

Read 2 Corinthians 12:9-10, implement the Four Basic Bible Study Steps, and record your responses and findings.

Step 1: PRAY

1. Begin by asking the Holy Spirit to guide you into all truth. Take a few minutes and write a prayer thanking God for His Word.

_____

_____

_____

_____

Step 2: OBSERVE

2 Corinthians 12:9-10

1. Who is speaking and being spoken to? Who is participating in the event? _____

_____

2. What is happening? What is being said? _____

_____

3. When is the event or conversation taking place? _____

_____

4. Where is the event or conversation taking place? _____

_____

5. Why is the event or conversation taking place? _____

_____

6. How is the event or conversation taking place?

_____

_____

7. Describe what you learned from this passage about where we receive our power.

_____

_____

_____

_____

_____

_____

_____

Step 3: INTERPRET

1. What does this text mean? What Timeless Life Lesson(s) do you believe God is trying to teach us?

_____

_____

_____

_____

Step 4: APPLY

1. What do you need to do? How will you specifically apply this lesson(s) to your life?

_____

_____

_____

_____

2. Journal additional thoughts God has placed on your heart regarding today's topic.

_____

_____

_____

_____

_____

_____

3. Write a prayer to God.

_____

_____

_____

_____

_____

_____

_____

Dear Friend and Courage Companion,

Although it's the end of our twelve-week journey together, the road to finding courage doesn't end here. Courage isn't a destination; it's a state of mind, heart, and spirit that is fueled and strengthened by the consistency of our willingness to make courageous choices based on scriptural truth each and every day.

Very few of us reach adulthood without carrying excess baggage of some sort—baggage that weighs us down and keeps us from fearlessly facing certain parts of our everyday life. However, with God's love, mercy, and infinite grace, we can lighten our load and learn to grasp a level of courage that will open our world to infinite possibilities.

My prayer for you is that your world has already begun to open up; that God has begun to show you how very special you are to Him. I pray you will never again hesitate to live life to the fullest, unleash your God-given courage, and allow God to unveil new chapters in your life—chapters you never dreamed were possible.

As I walked my own journey to find courage, I never imagined having the life I now live. It's a life I've dedicated to the pursuit of knowing God intimately and sharing His love, mercy, and grace with people just like you. I invite you to stay connected with me and my ministry and let me know how you are doing.

Over time, I'll be providing new resources for continued Bible study, including live, online interactive studies and special events. Please make sure to subscribe to my devotions, podcasts, and Bible reading plans and bookmark my website so you can visit often.

In closing, I wish you much success as you take on new challenges and face life with unending courage and unwavering faith!

May God Bless you & Strengthen you always!

LESSON 12

REVIEW

COURAGE QUOTE

True joy is a product of comfort in the midst of crisis, trust in the midst of uncertainty, and hope in the midst of all circumstances.

COURAGE VERSE

Now may the God of hope fill you with all joy and peace in believing, so that you will abound in hope by the power of the Holy Spirit.

–Romans 15:13

Timeless Life Lessons Learned

APPENDIX

LEADER GUIDE

COURAGE FOR LIFE LEADER GUIDE

Thank you for accepting the call to lead this twelve-week *Courage For Life* study. No matter your stage on your personal courage journey, you can rest assured God will equip and enable you to accomplish this courageous task. As God prepares you, we want to come along side you to offer encouragement and support.

The following guidelines have been prepared with both you and your group in mind. They are intended to enhance your group's experience and help every group participant (GP) reach his/her courage journey potential. We have based the following principles on *proven practices* that foster a safe, healthy, non-judgmental environment and encourage participation and interaction, an environment where all members can find hope, healing, and courage.

As a group leader (GL), your role is to encourage and motivate the GPs throughout the learning process and to facilitate group discussions in a way that creates a safe sharing environment. Be sure to visit CourageForLife.org/Leader for access to additional resources.

PLEASE NOTE: This group should in no way seek to take the place of professional or legal counseling.

Leading a Group

1. Make sure you, and every GP, has a copy of the book *Courage For Life* ® and a copy of this *Courage For Life Study Guide*.

2. Schedule weekly meetings in a relaxed, safe sharing environment.

3. Allow approximately two hours for a group meeting. This allows time for fellowship, prayer, and at least one hour or more for the lesson discussion.

4. Ahead of time, prepare a list of open-ended questions related to each week's lesson that will encourage participants to openly share with the group.

5. Make it a goal to begin and end group meetings promptly at the scheduled time and include an opening and closing prayer.

6. Request all cell phones be turned off or silenced. If a participant needs to take a call or return a text, encourage him/her to leave the room so other members are not distracted.

7. Inform participants that photos or any form of audio/visual recording is prohibited, a rule which will foster a safe and confidential environment.

8. Encourage GPs to attend all meetings on time. This will help your group develop strong, trusting relationships.

9. Review the Recommended Group Discussion Guidelines (on the next page) with GPs and go over them at the beginning of your first group meeting. You can download a PDF version handout of these guidelines by going to CourageForLife.org/GroupGuidelines.

10. Be available before and after class to fellowship with participants, but maintain healthy boundaries regarding your time.

11. Ask questions and listen carefully to individual responses. Encourage the other GPs to listen attentively and affirm each person's participation.

12. Maintain control of the group and offer structure, strength, and hope. Stay on topic and don't allow any GP to dominate the conversation or discussion. Consider setting a time limit of one to two minutes for responses and personal stories, if necessary.

13. Be structured but flexible. Allow for times when a participant's questions or responses will require additional clarity or group discussion.

14. Don't be afraid of silence. Allow people time to gain the courage to share and make sure you and your GPs are allowing everyone an opportunity to share.

15. Refer GPs to visit CourageForLife.org where they can download "Available Charts and Resources." Encourage them to sign up for our weekly devotions and make sure to invite them to follow Courage For Life on Facebook, Twitter, Instagram, and Pinterest for daily encouragement.

Recommended Group Discussion Guidelines

1. Participate and share at your own comfort level while working toward becoming more courageously open and transparent with the group.

2. Refrain from giving advice. Instead, share from your own experiences and offer a listening ear and a willingness to pray.

3. Refrain from interrupting when others are sharing.

4. Maintain a non-judgmental attitude at all times, toward group participants as well as people outside of the group.

5. Memorize this foundational statement:

   "I cannot change another person by direct action. I can only change myself. Others tend to change in reaction to my change."

6. Always respect the confidentiality of the group. This will foster an environment of comfort and safety that encourages spiritual, personal, and relational growth.

Dear Leader,

Thank you again for accepting the call to lead a *Courage For Life* group study! We are praying for you and excited about all God will do in your life and in the lives of your group members as you begin your *Courage For Life* journey together.

Be strong & courageous!
God is with you wherever you go!

RECOMMENDED RESOURCES FOR INDUCTIVE BIBLE STUDY

Helpful Guidebooks on Purchasing Commentaries

- *Old Testament Commentary Survey*, 5th Edition, Grand Rapids, MI: Baker Academic
- *New Testament Commentary Survey*, 7th Edition, Grand Rapids, MI: Baker Academic

Recommended Commentaries

- *The New American Commentary* [NAC], Nashville, TN: Broadman and Holman Publishers, 1991
- *The Bible Knowledge Commentary: An Exposition of the Scriptures,* Wheaton, IL: Victor Books
- *The NIV Application Commentary,* Grand Rapids, MI: Zondervan Publishing House

Old and New Testament Introductions

- *The World and the Word: An Introduction to the Old Testament,* Nashville, TN: B&H Publishing
- *The Lion and the Lamb: New Testament Essentials from the Cradle, the Cross, and the Crown,* Nashville, TN: B&H Publishing

Bible Atlases

- *Holman Bible Atlas,* Nashville, TN: B&H Publishing
- *Crossway ESV Bible Atlas*, Wheaton, IL: Crossway Publishers

Bible Dictionaries

- *Holman Illustrated Bible Dictionary,* Nashville, TN: Broadman and Holman Publishers
- *Eerdmans Bible Dictionary,* Grand Rapids, MI: Wm. B. Eerdmans Publishing Company

Bible Encyclopedias

- *International Standard Bible Encyclopedia,* Grand Rapids, MI: Wm. B. Eerdmans Publishing Company
- *The Zondervan Pictorial Bible Encyclopedia,* Grand Rapids, MI: Zondervan Publishing House

Study Bibles

- *English Standard Version Study Bible,* Wheaton, Ill: Crossway Publishers
- *Holman Christian Standard Bible,* Nashville, TN: Holman Bible Publishers
- *New American Standard Bible,* Eugene, OR: Harvest House Publishers

Bible Software

- Accordance
- Bible Works
- Logos
- Word Search

Currently Available Online Resources

- **BibleMesh.com**: Offers affordable and quality Bible education.
- **BibleGateway.com**: Search for verses and compare translations.
- **Preceptaustin.org**: Find a variety of resources on Bible study and Bible topics.
- **Radical.net**: Read resources written by David Platt and his team.
- **TrueLife.org**: Find biblical answers to difficult questions.
- **thegospelcoalition.org**: Read articles that elevate the gospel in principle and practice.
- **wacriswell.org**: Read sermons and resources by W.A. Criswell.
- **desiringgod.org**: Find resources and sermons by John Piper.
- **gty.org**: Find resources and sermons by John MacArthur.
- **9marks.org**: Read articles and book reviews written by a team of evangelical Christians.
- **spurgeongems.org**: Read Charles Spurgeon's sermons and resources.
- **DanielAkin.com**: Read Daniel Akin's sermons and resources.
- **Bible.org**: Read articles and utilize resources written by a team of evangelical Christians.
- **probe.org**: Discover articles written on a variety of topics.
- **4truth.net**: Learn more about how to defend your faith.

AUDACIA PARA VIVIR

The inspiring book, *Courage For Life,* is also available in Spanish!

For more information or to purchase your copy of *Courage For Life* in Spanish, visit:

CourageForLife.org/Espanol

FREE E-BOOK AND RESOURCES

30 Days of Courage

We would love to invest in you. So we're offering our *30 Days of Courage* e-book absolutely free. Our hope is that it will motivate you to continue to implement courage from God into every aspect of your life. From personal relationships to professional endeavors, from unfailing faith to bountiful forgiveness, from the ability to persevere to the fearless pursuit of your God-given dreams. This devotional will inspire you to set aside your fears and inject bravery into your everyday life.

To download your free copy of *30 Days of Courage,* visit:

CourageForLife.org/Free

Online Resources

Strengthen your courage walk by downloading the charts referenced from the *Courage For Life* book.

To access your free online resources from *Courage For Life,* visit:

CourageForLife.org/Free

SHARE YOUR THOUGHTS
AND STAY CONNECTED

- Join an online Bible study.

- Access free resources.

- Sign up to receive our devotional, "Inspiration For Life."

- Add your prayer requests to our prayer wall.

- E-mail comments and questions to: Contact@CourageForLife.org.

Let us hear from you!

CourageForLife.org

To inquire about having Ann speak at your event, visit or e-mail:

AnnWhite.com

Info@AnnWhite.com

HOW TO STUDY THE BIBLE
WITH COURAGE AND CONFIDENCE

Do you want to know God more personally, understand His Word more extensively, and apply His truth more effectively?

How to Study the Bible with Courage and Confidence by Ann White is designed to help you:

- Learn practical, easy steps to implement when studying the Bible.
- Unlock truth for yourself—book by book.
- Understand what you are reading and discover timeless life lessons.
- Unearth God's practical advice for your everyday life.
- Apply life-changing truth to your ever-changing circumstances.
- Discover inner peace beyond your imagination.

Ann White knows what it's like to go from a life of self-reliance to one full of hope, courage, and confidence, empowered by a personal relationship with God and life lessons from His Word. She wants this for you too.

For more information or to purchase your copy of
How to Study the Bible with Courage and Confidence, visit:

CourageForLife.org/HowToStudyTheBible

Perfect for Individuals and Small Groups!

ABOUT ANN WHITE

Ann is a native Carolina girl who met her husband and soul mate shortly after moving to Atlanta in 1978. She founded Courage For Life, out of a calling to share with others how God and His Word brought restoration to her life and marriage. Ann is an internationally known author, speaker, and passionate Bible teacher.

For years, Ann's heart has been burdened for those who need to hear God's Word and are suffering due to circumstances beyond their control. Having personally experienced God's grace, salvation, and the life-changing power of the Bible, Ann's desire is to extend this same love, mercy, and encouragement to others, so they too may be reconciled to God.

Despite her busy schedule, most days you can find Ann spending quiet moments with the Lord, hanging out with her husband, boys, and their families, writing, reading, enjoying dear friends, and encouraging everyone she meets to embrace COURAGE FOR LIFE. She prays you will join her.

CourageForLife.org

COURAGE
FOR LIFE

ABOUT COURAGE FOR LIFE

Courage For Life leads people to unleash their God-given courage and embrace their God-given dreams.

Too many of us go through life pretending we have it all together. Ann and the team at Courage For Life are passionate about sharing their personal journeys of courage and redemption to equip individuals to have the courage not to settle in life. They lead Courage For Life studies and conferences both domestically and internationally. Through books, Bible studies, and teaching resources, the Courage For Life team is dedicated to helping others:

- find the courage to change
- develop the courage to lead
- have the courage to serve

Because they believe God's Word is central in finding courage, Courage For Life desires to equip believers to be better students and teachers of the Bible. And while it's their primary objective to see individuals have the courage to change their own life, they realize the benefits of that change are never exclusively for the individual, but for the common good of all people and for the glory of God.

If you are for COURAGE and want to partner with Ann and the Courage For Life team, join their Champions for Courage monthly giving society and receive your Welcome Kit, which includes a copy of Ann's latest book, and receive their weekly "Inspiration For Life" devotions along with regular ministry updates by visiting CourageForLife.org/GivingSociety.

Courage For Life is a 501(c)(3) public charity. As such, your gift of support is deductible as allowed by law.

CourageForLife.org
Contact@CourageForLife.org

1000 Whitlock Ave., Suite 320-134, Marietta, GA 30064
EXPLORE ADDITIONAL BOOKS and STUDY GUIDES by ANN WHITE

JOURNAL